Butterfly in the Garden

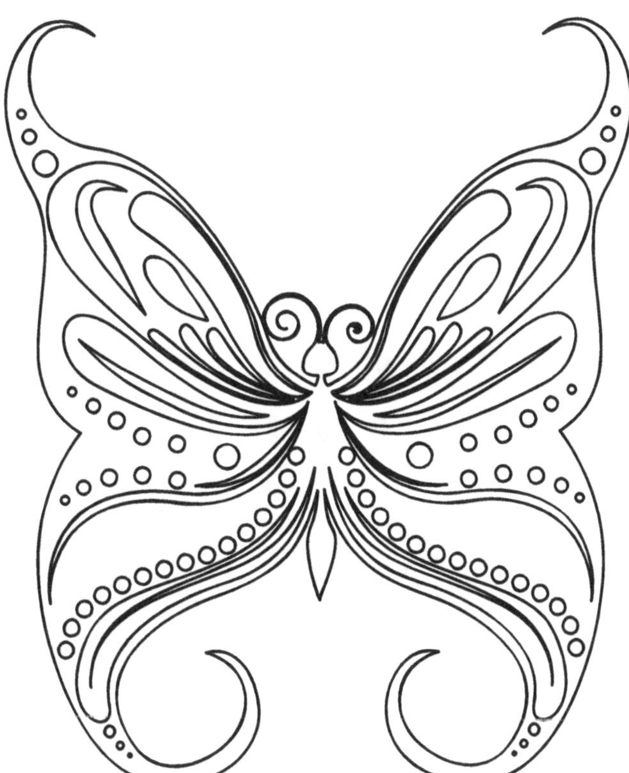

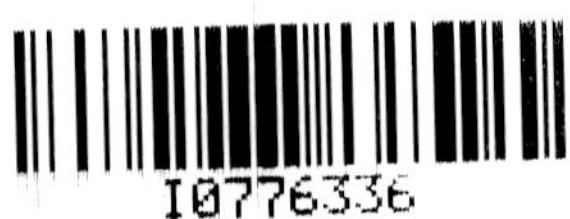

Adult Coloring Book

Oancea Camelia

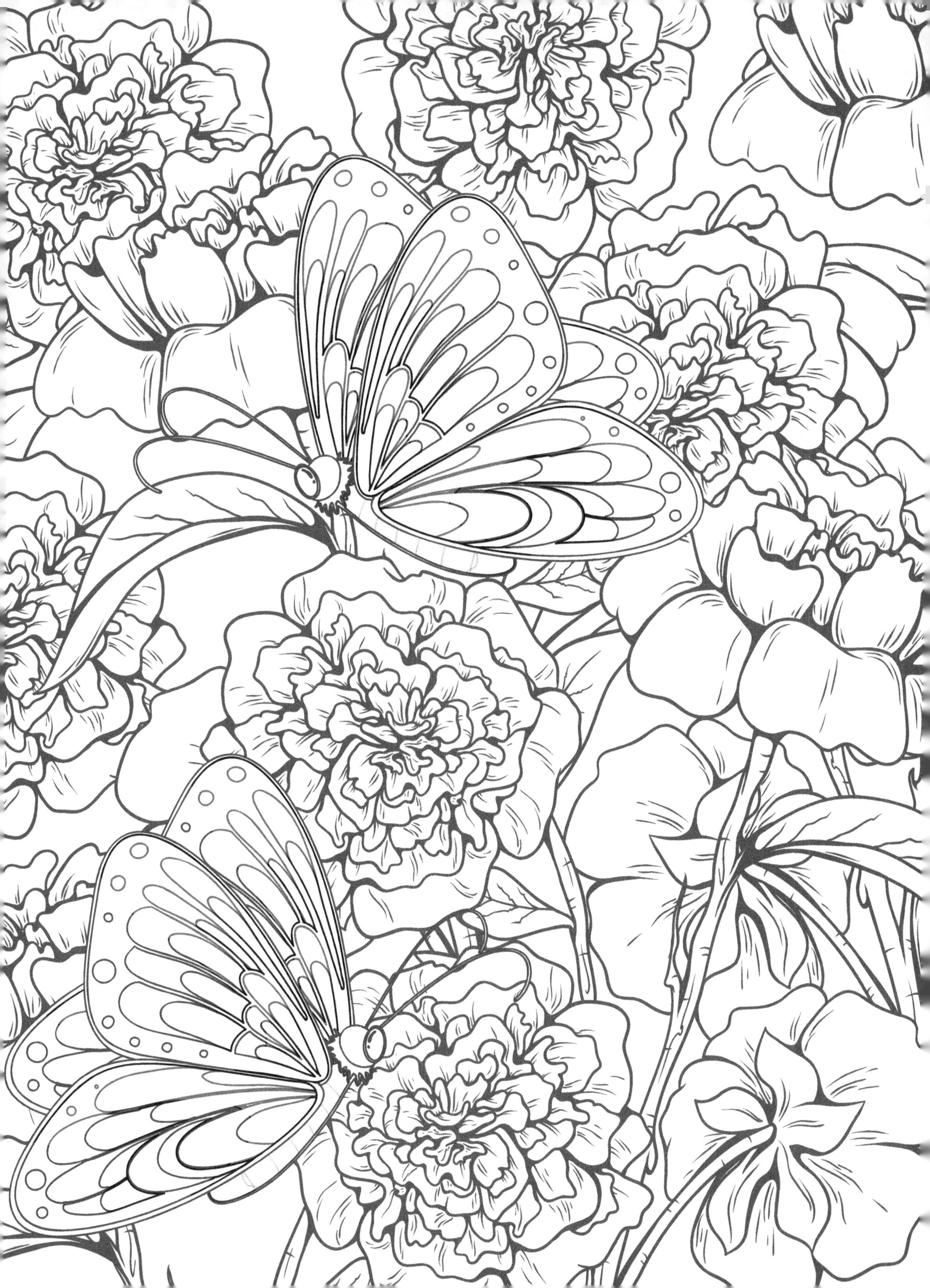

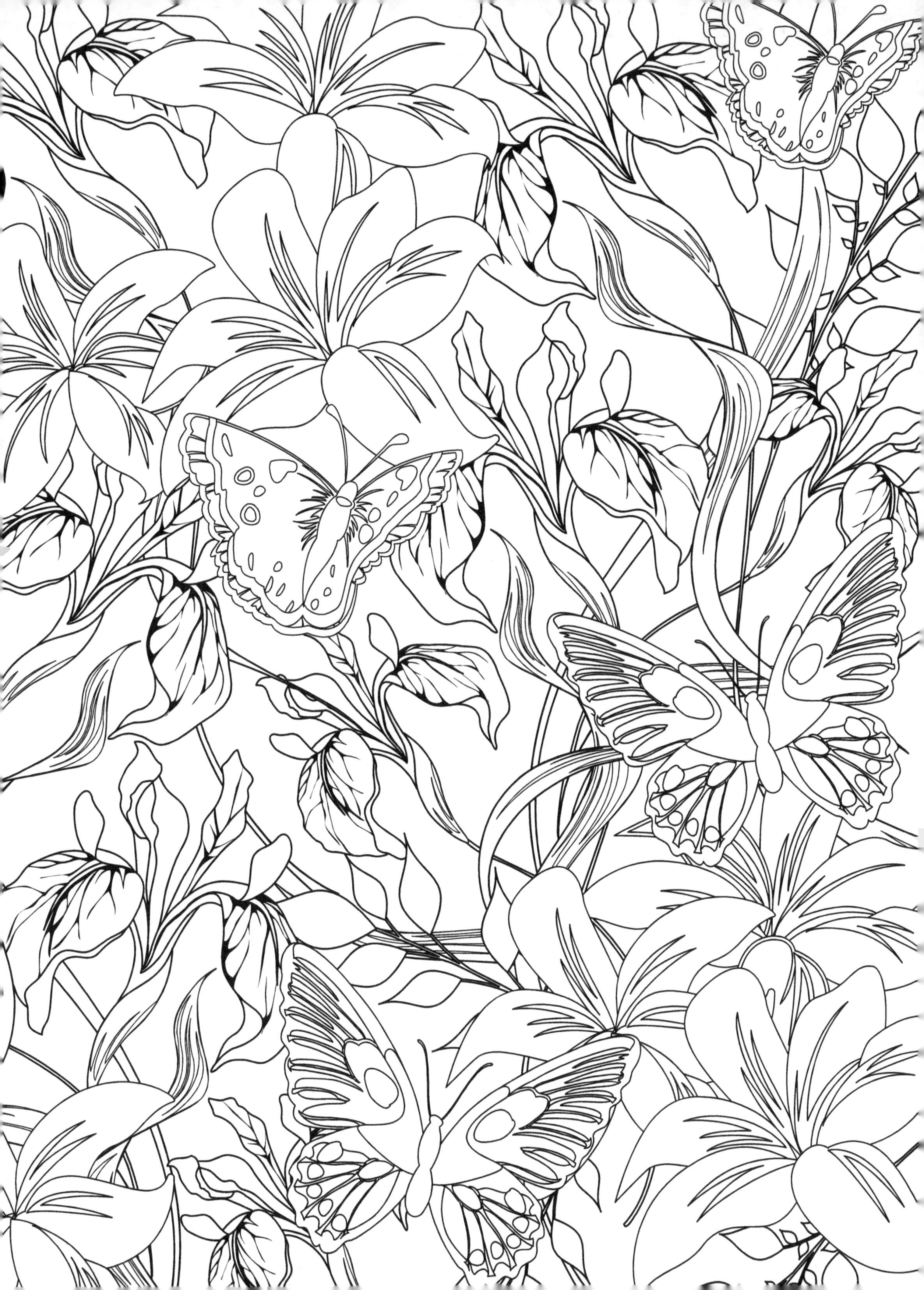

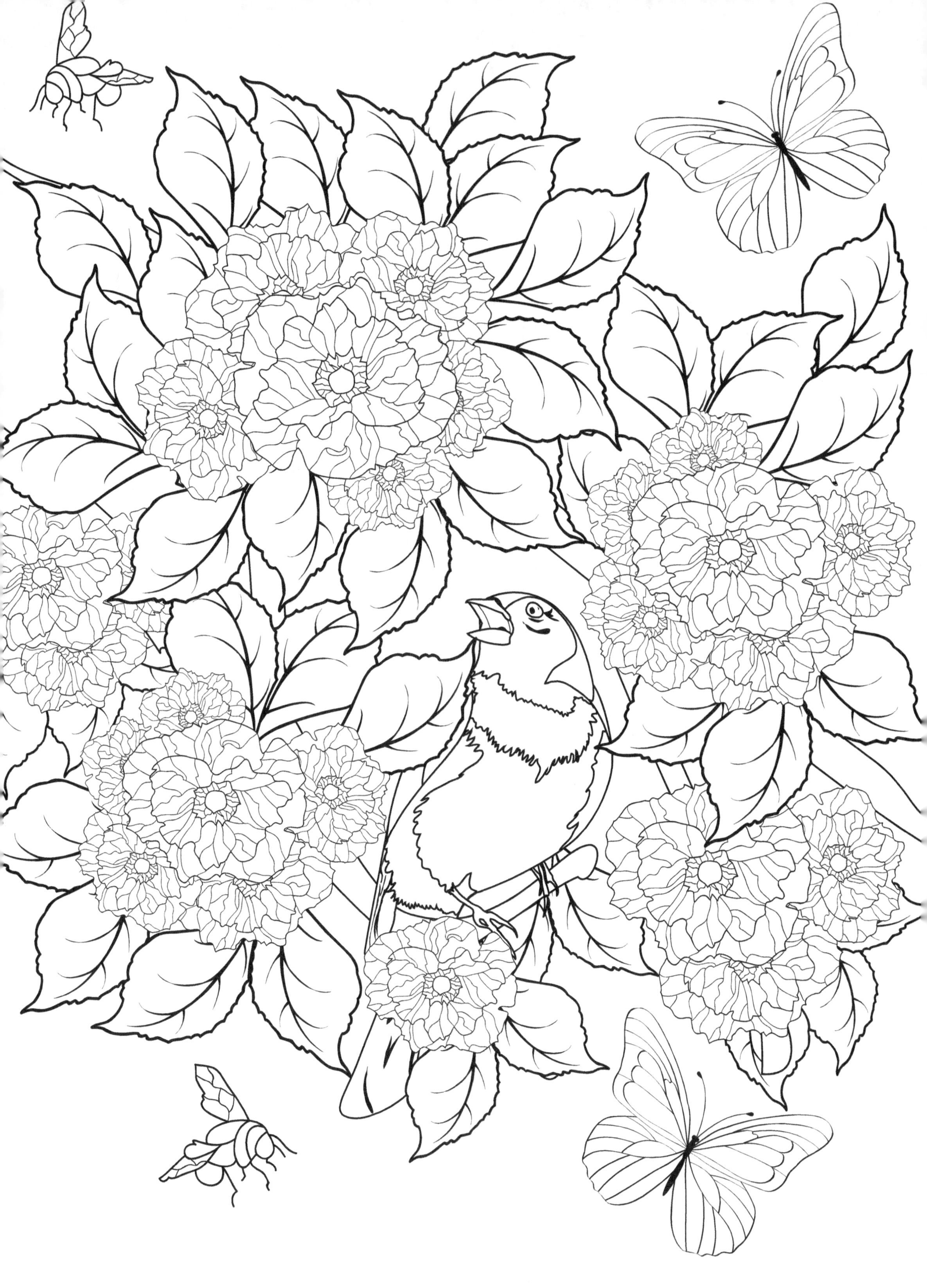

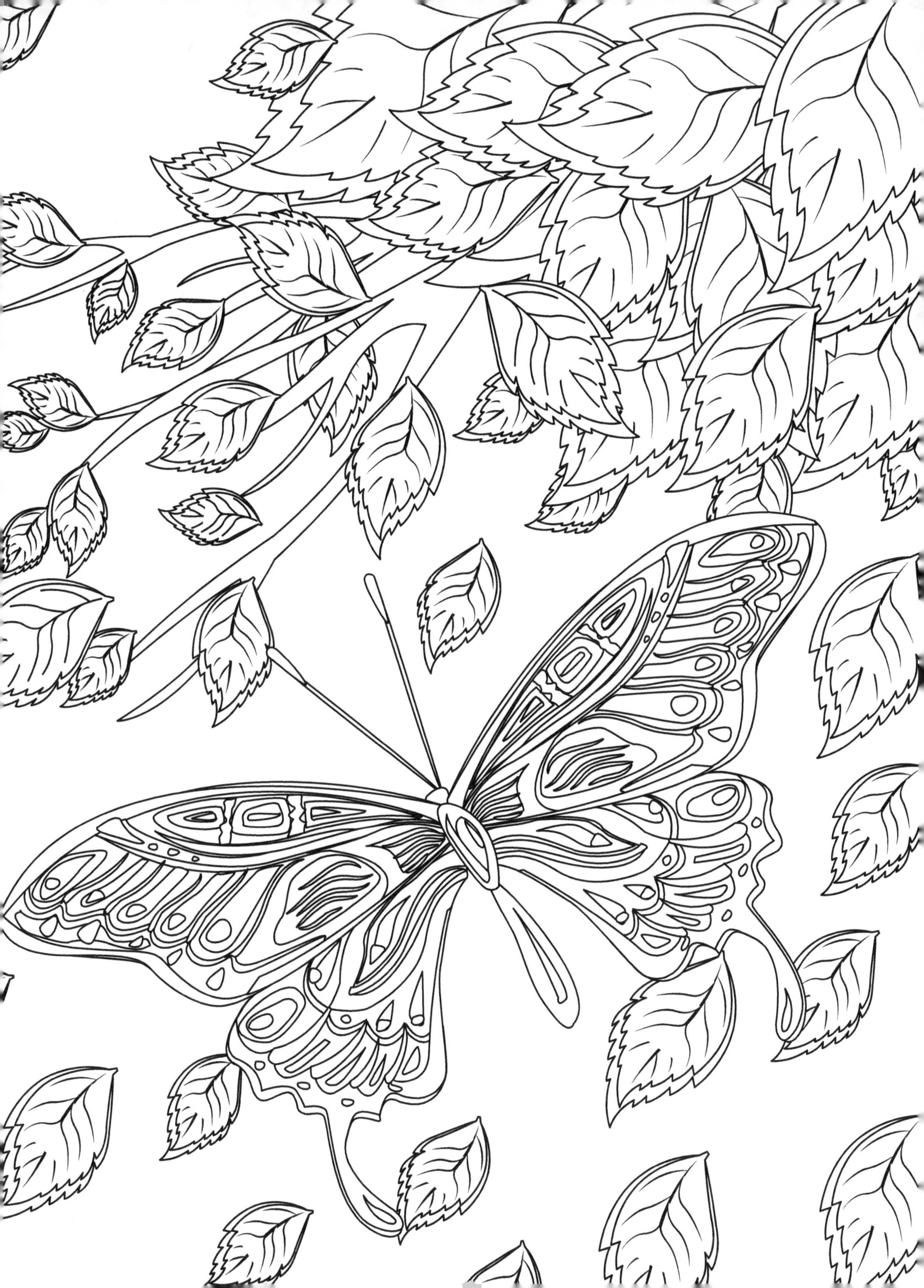

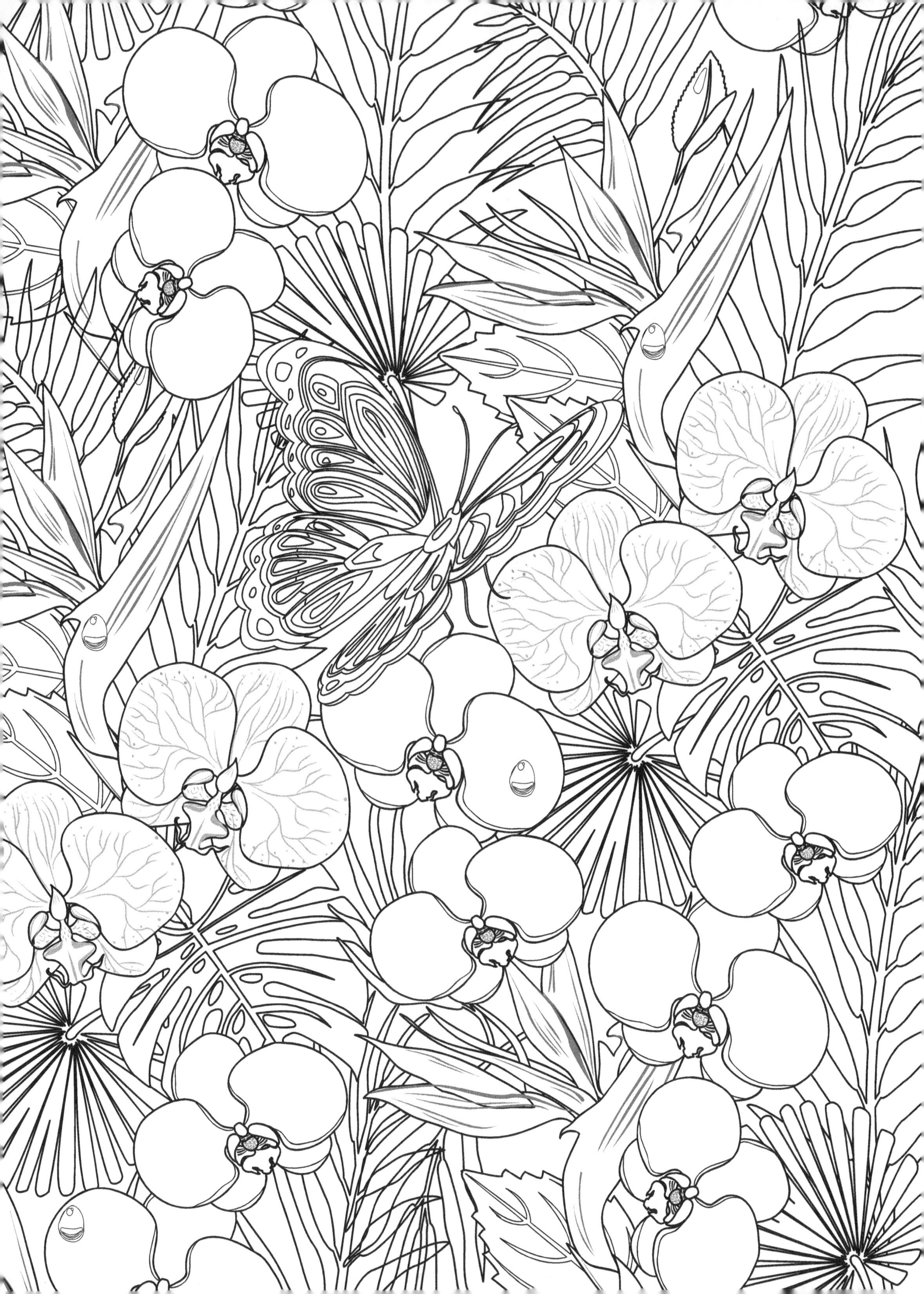

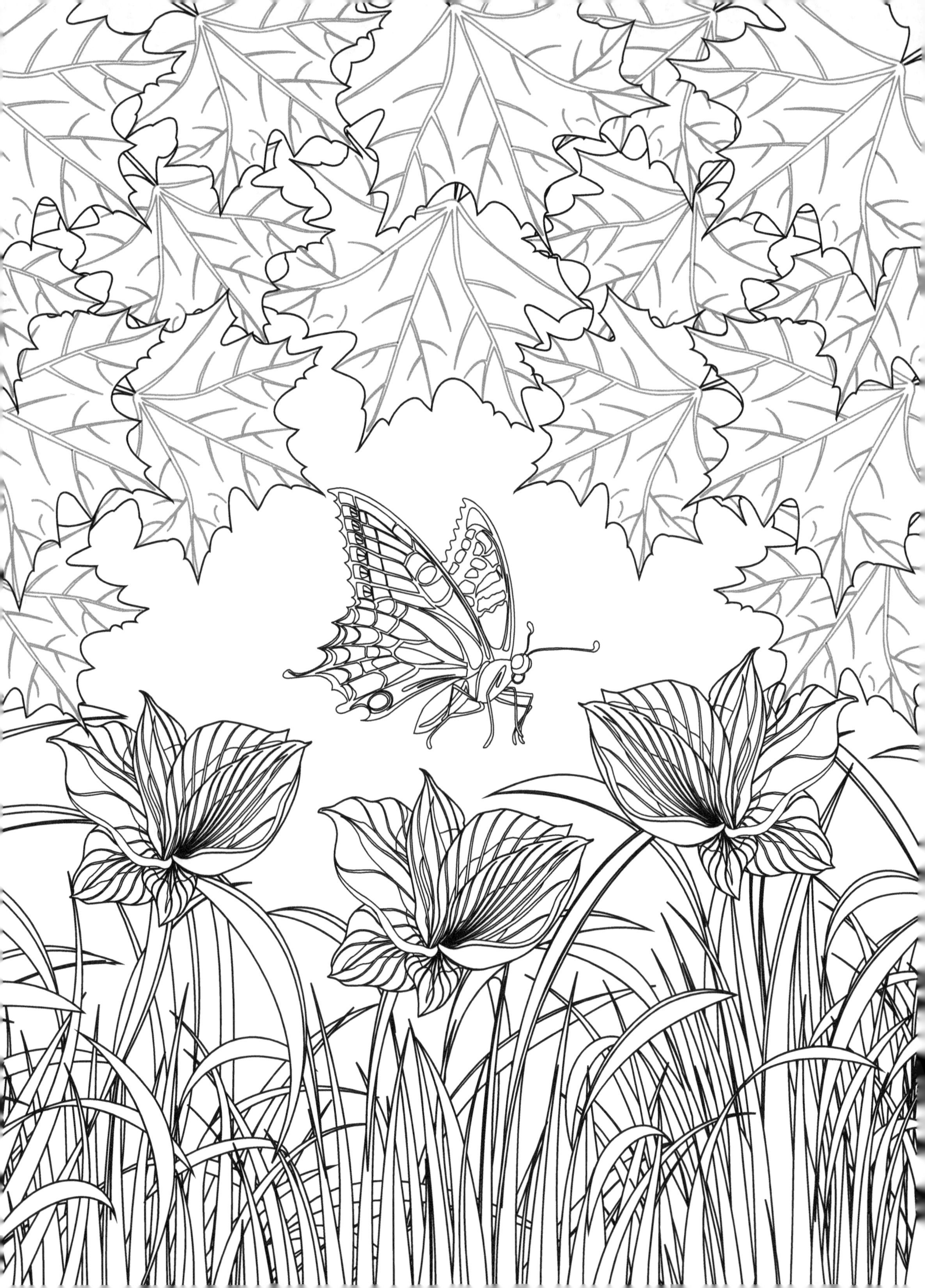

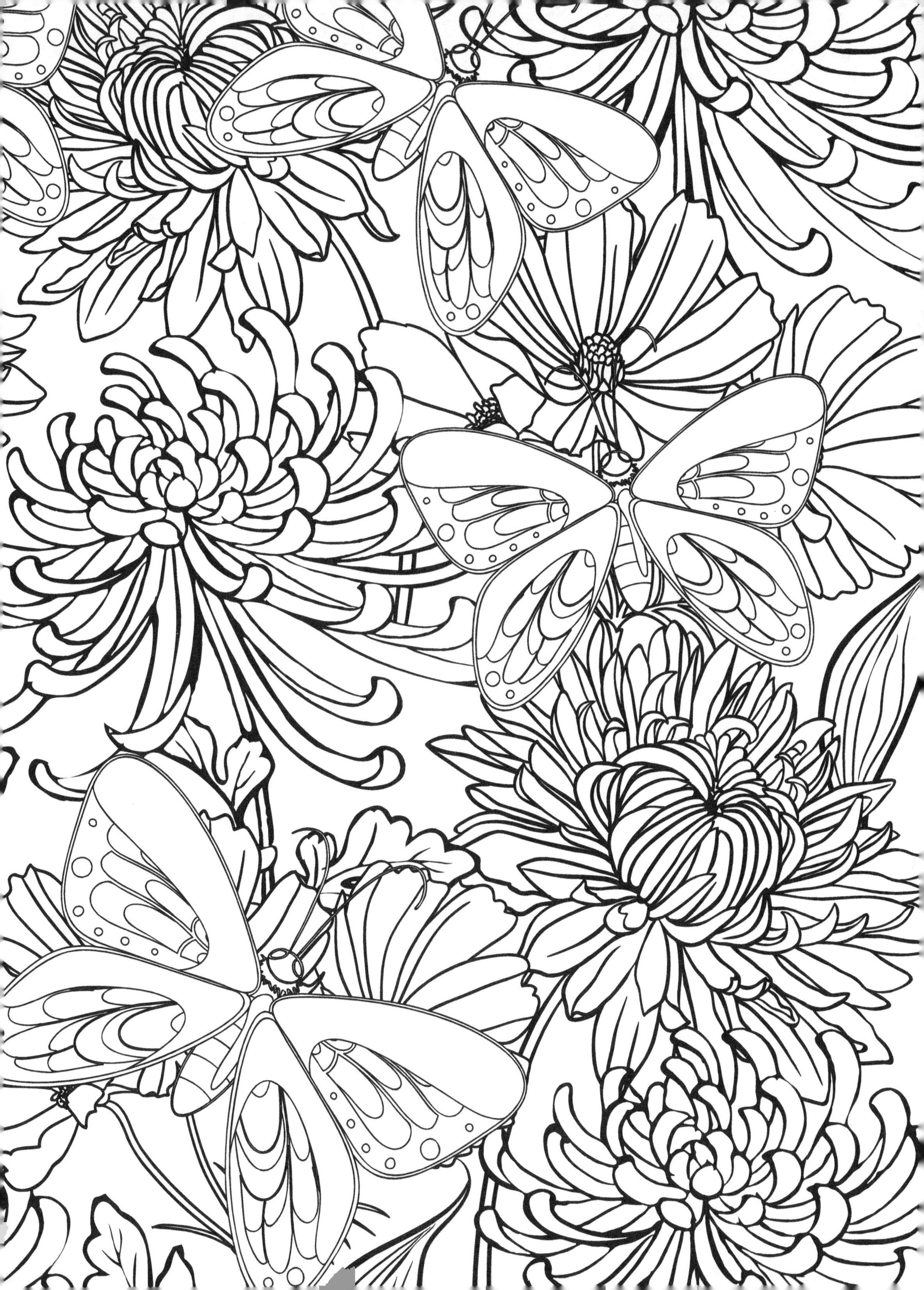

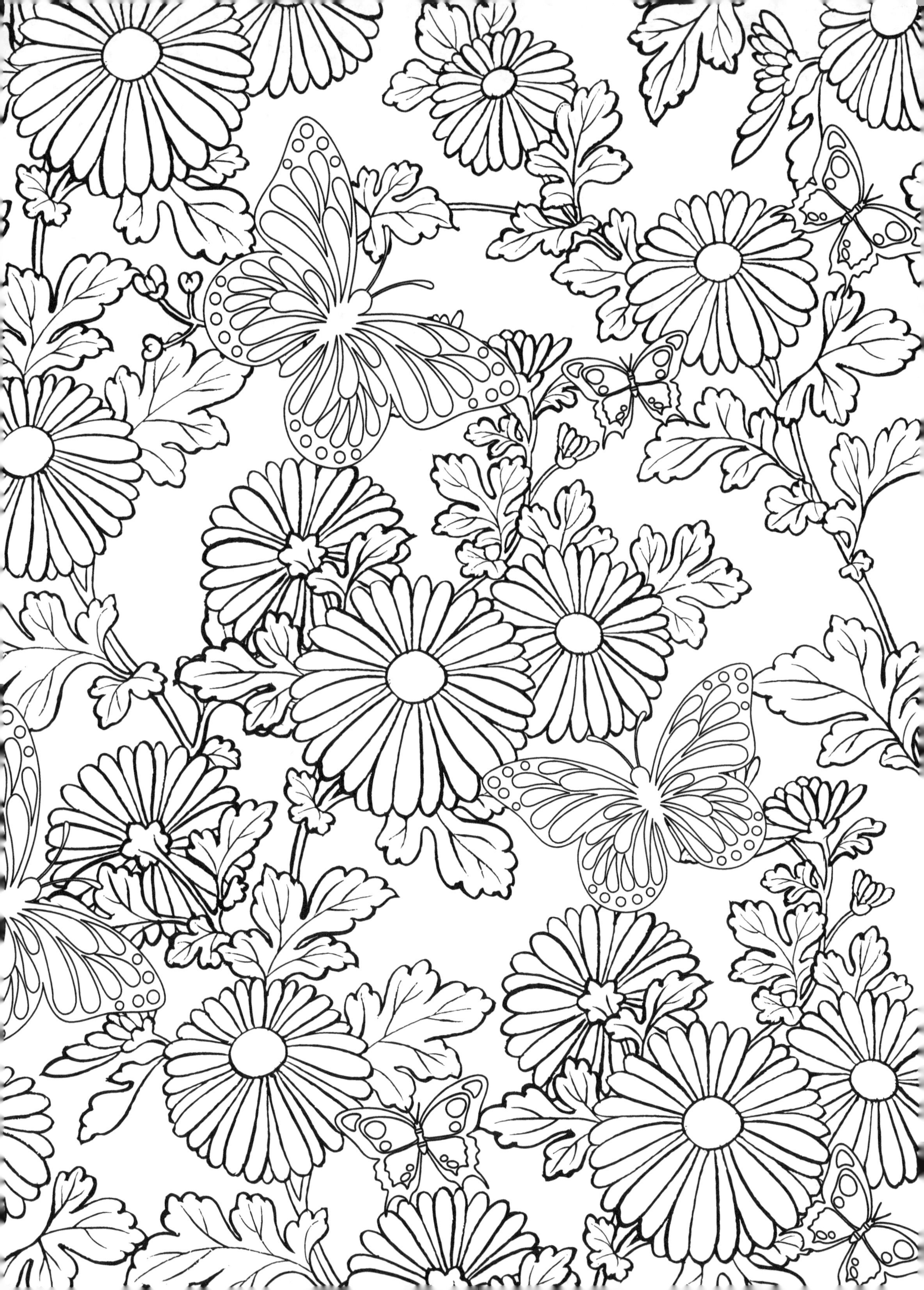

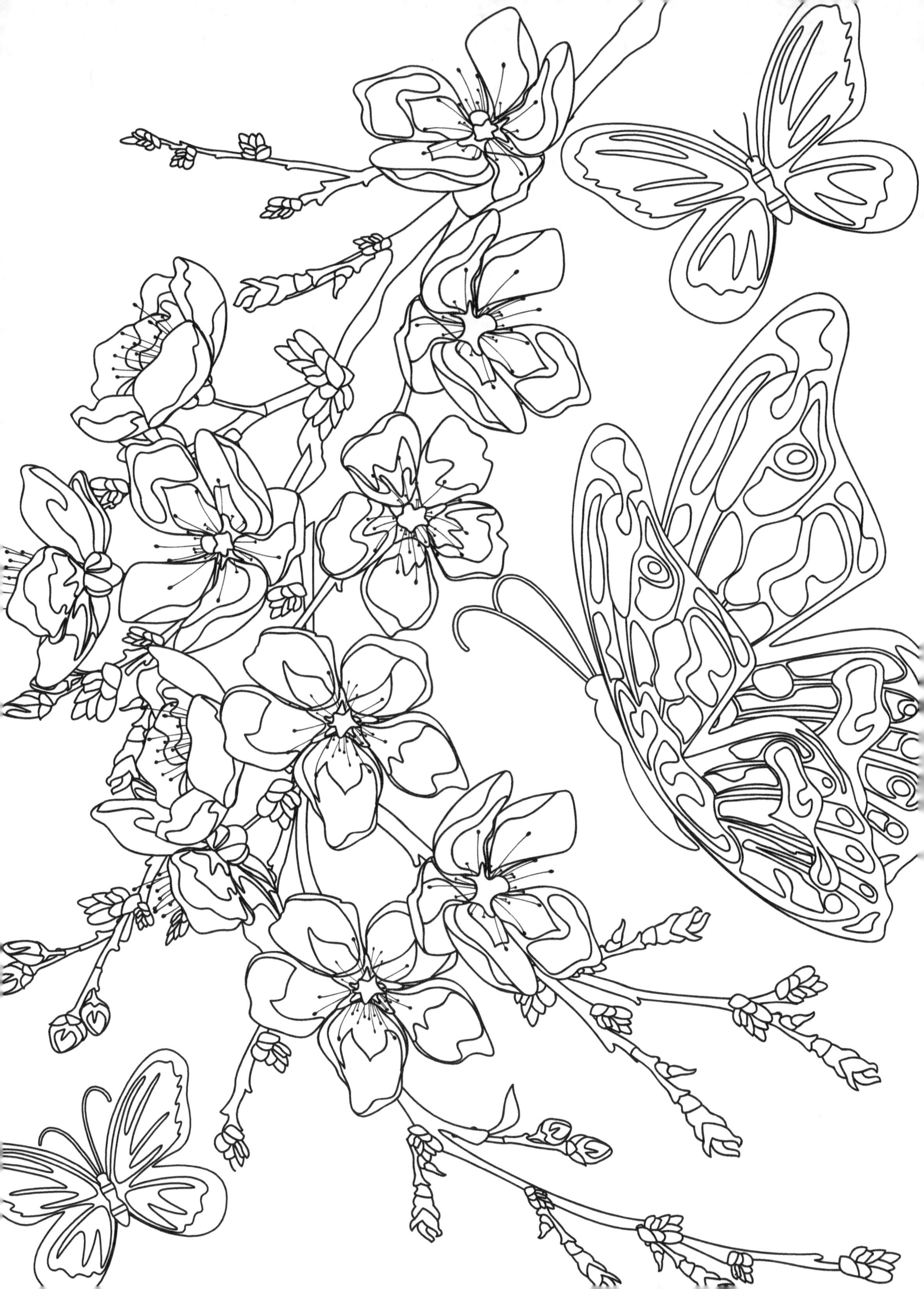

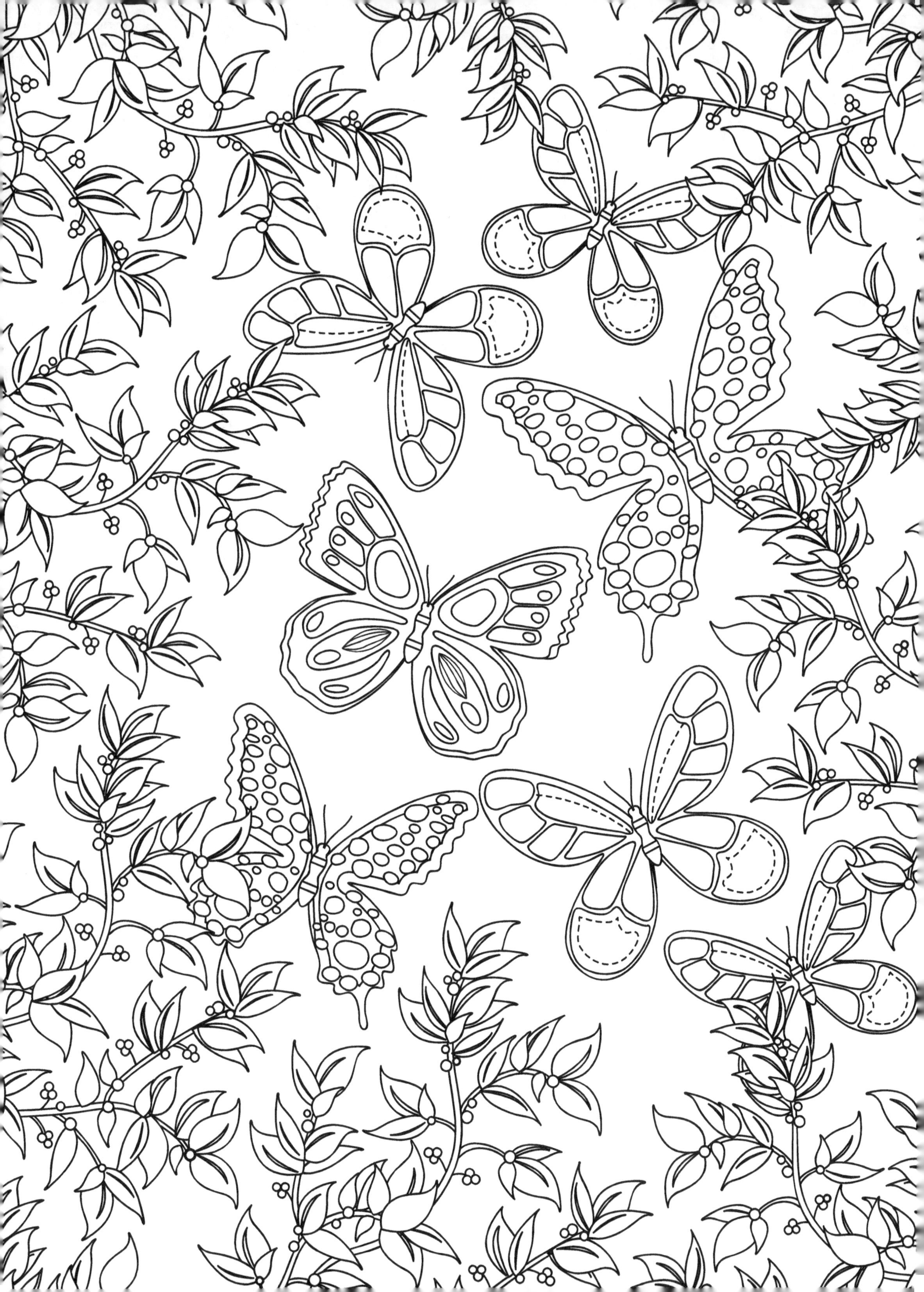

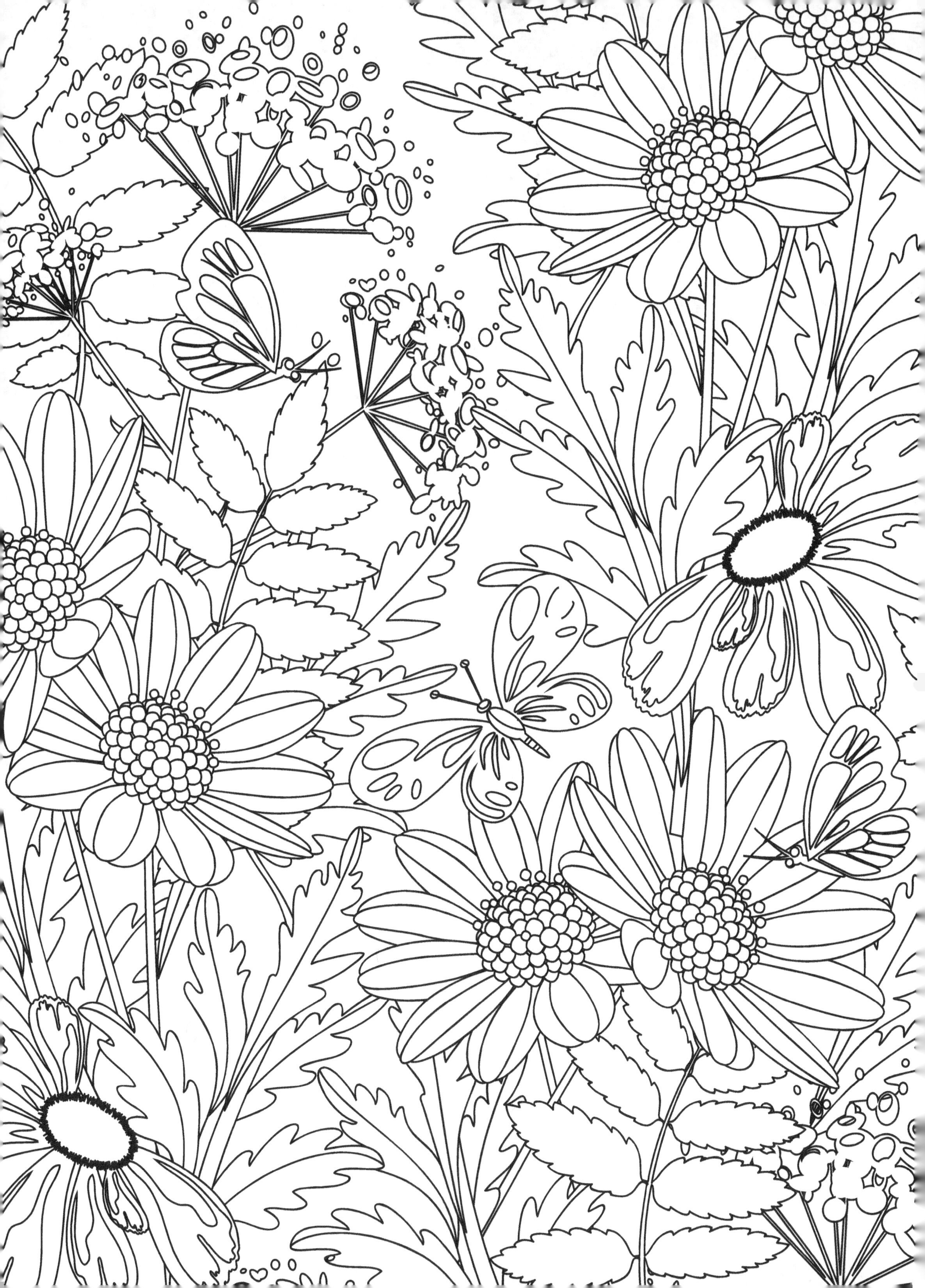

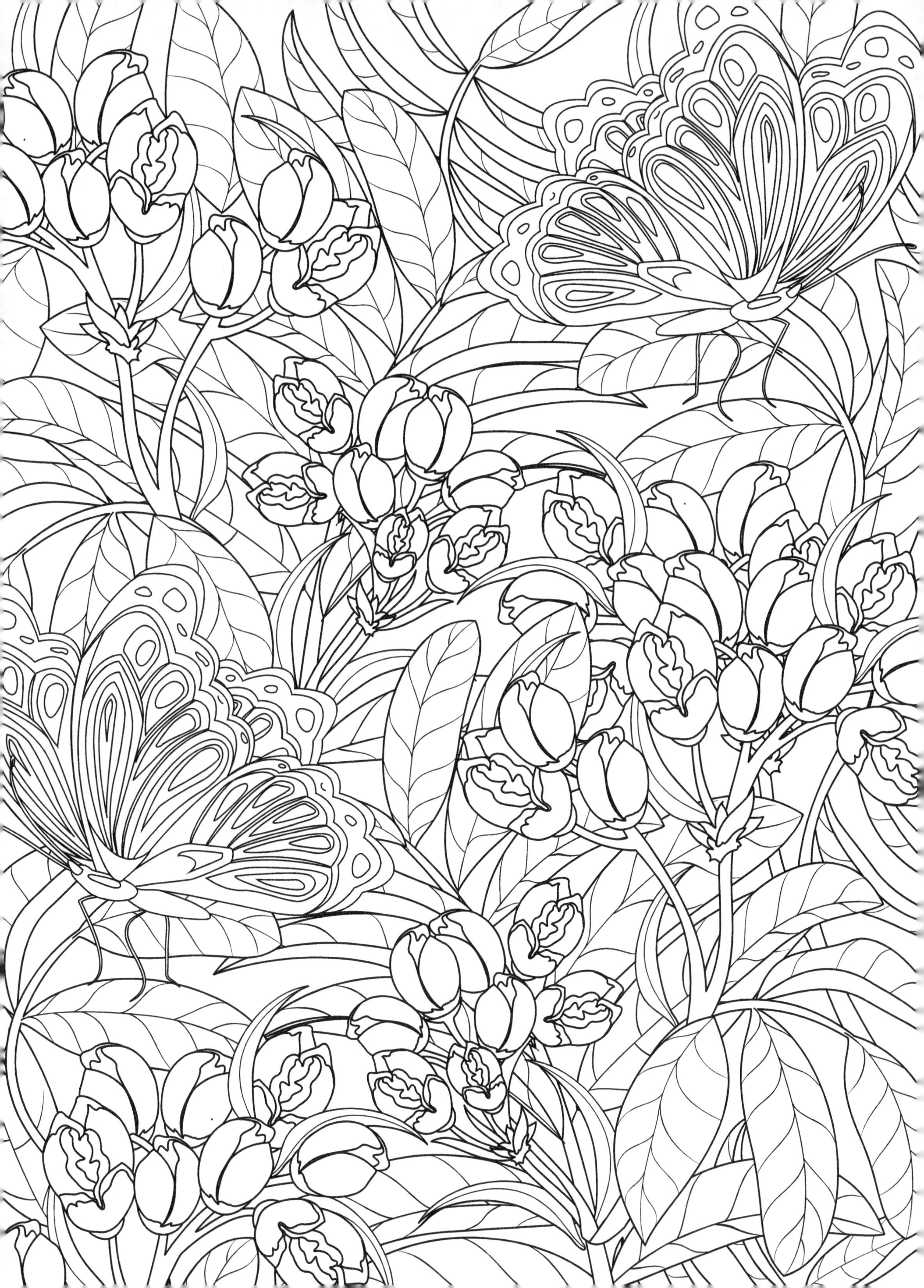

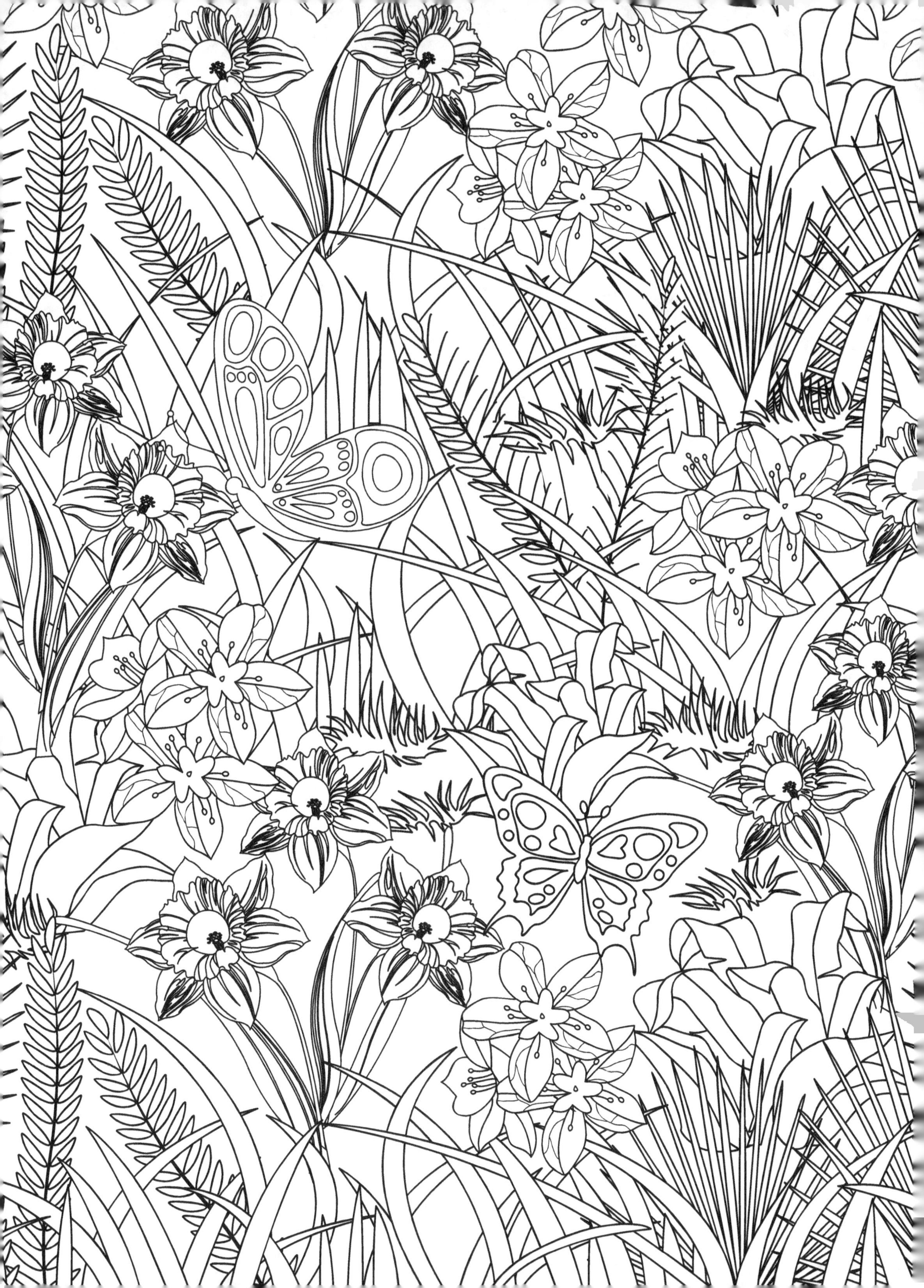

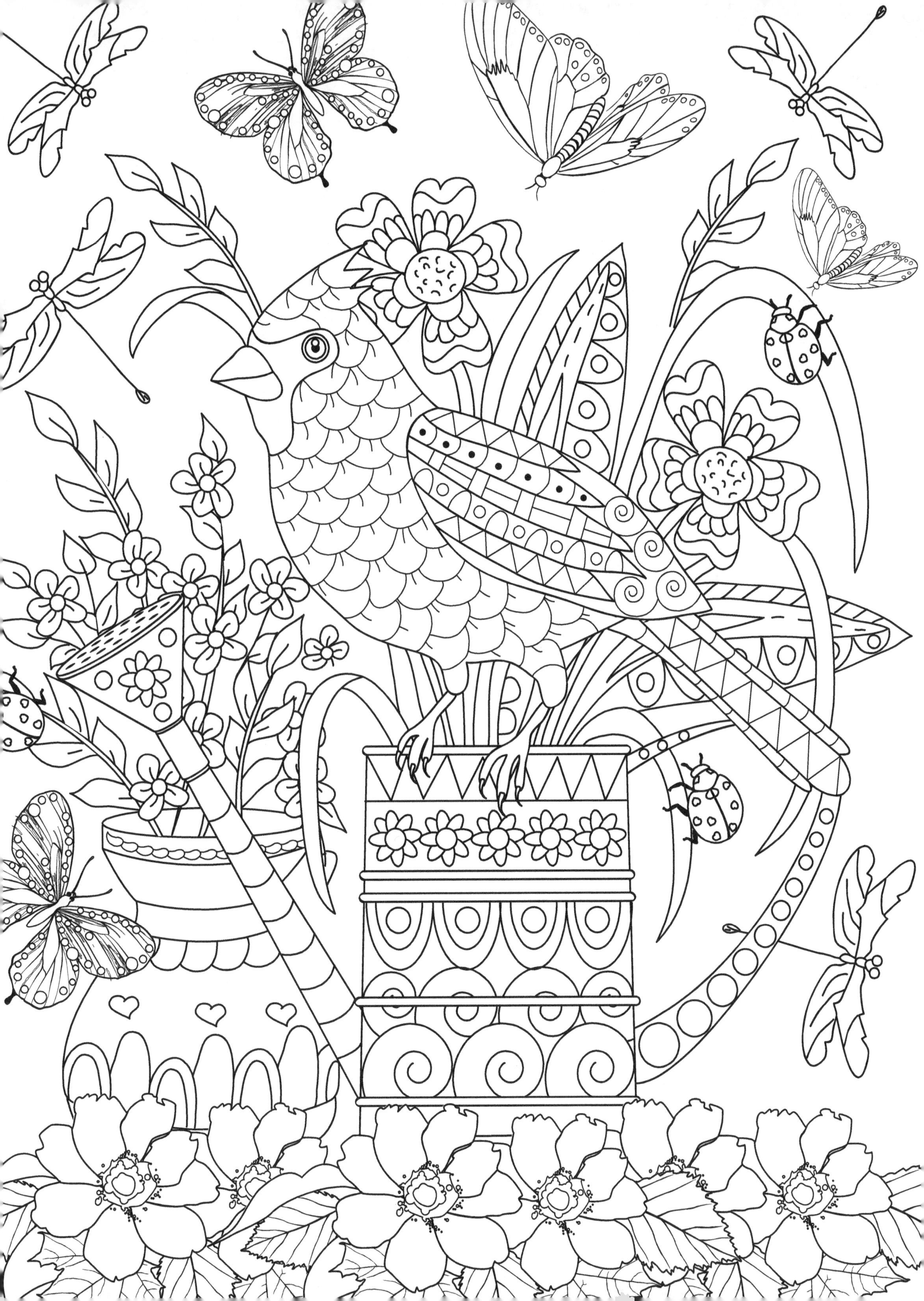

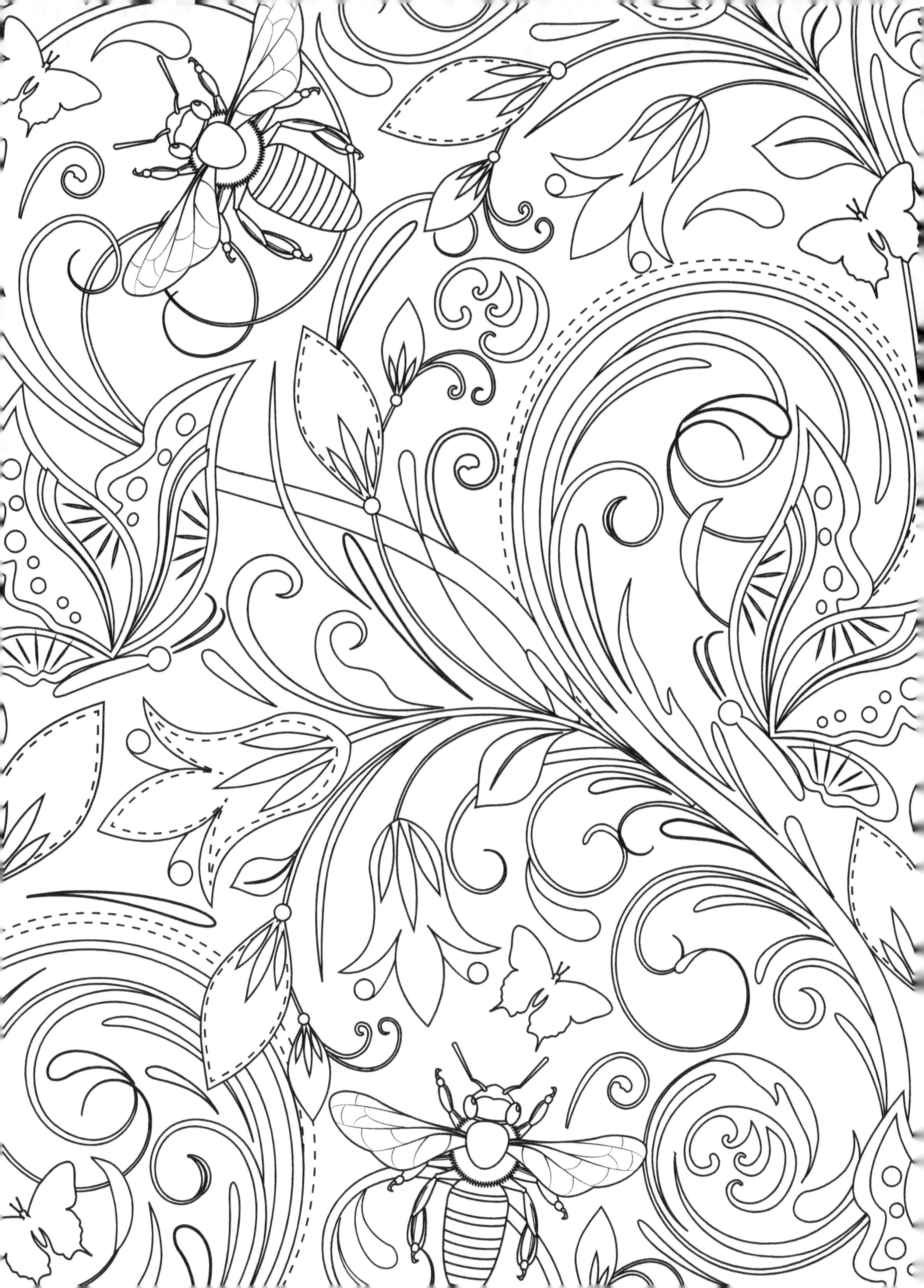

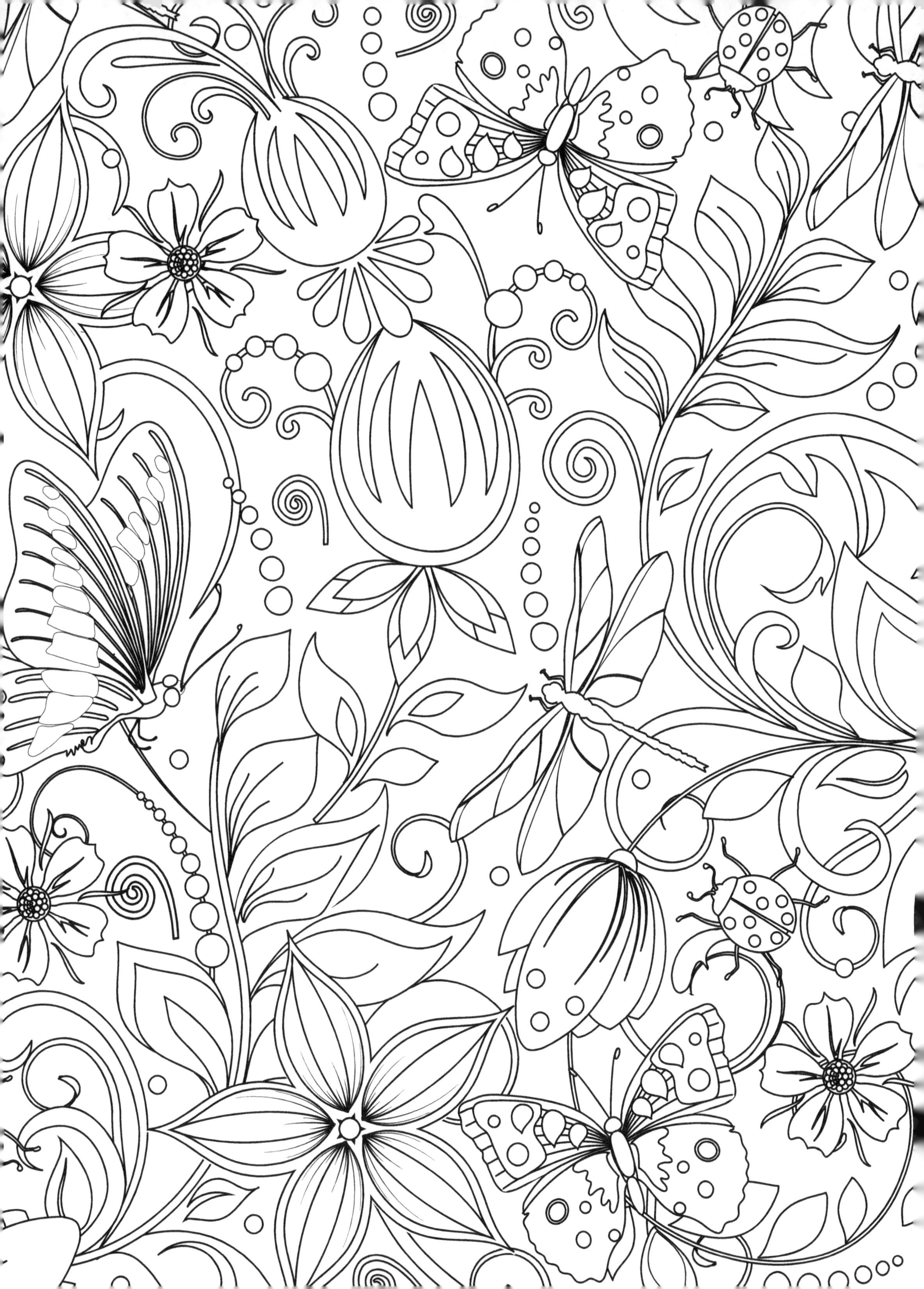

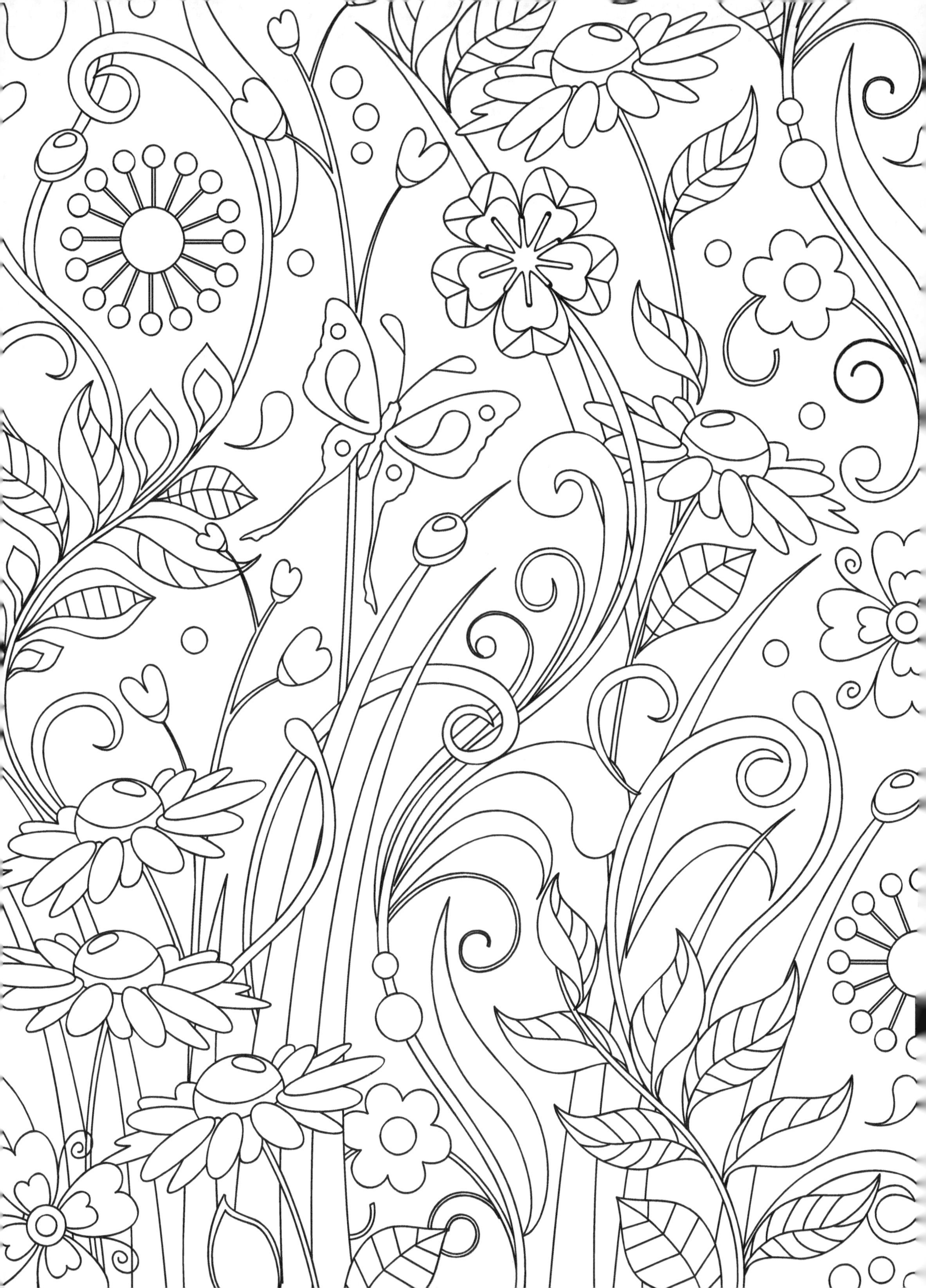

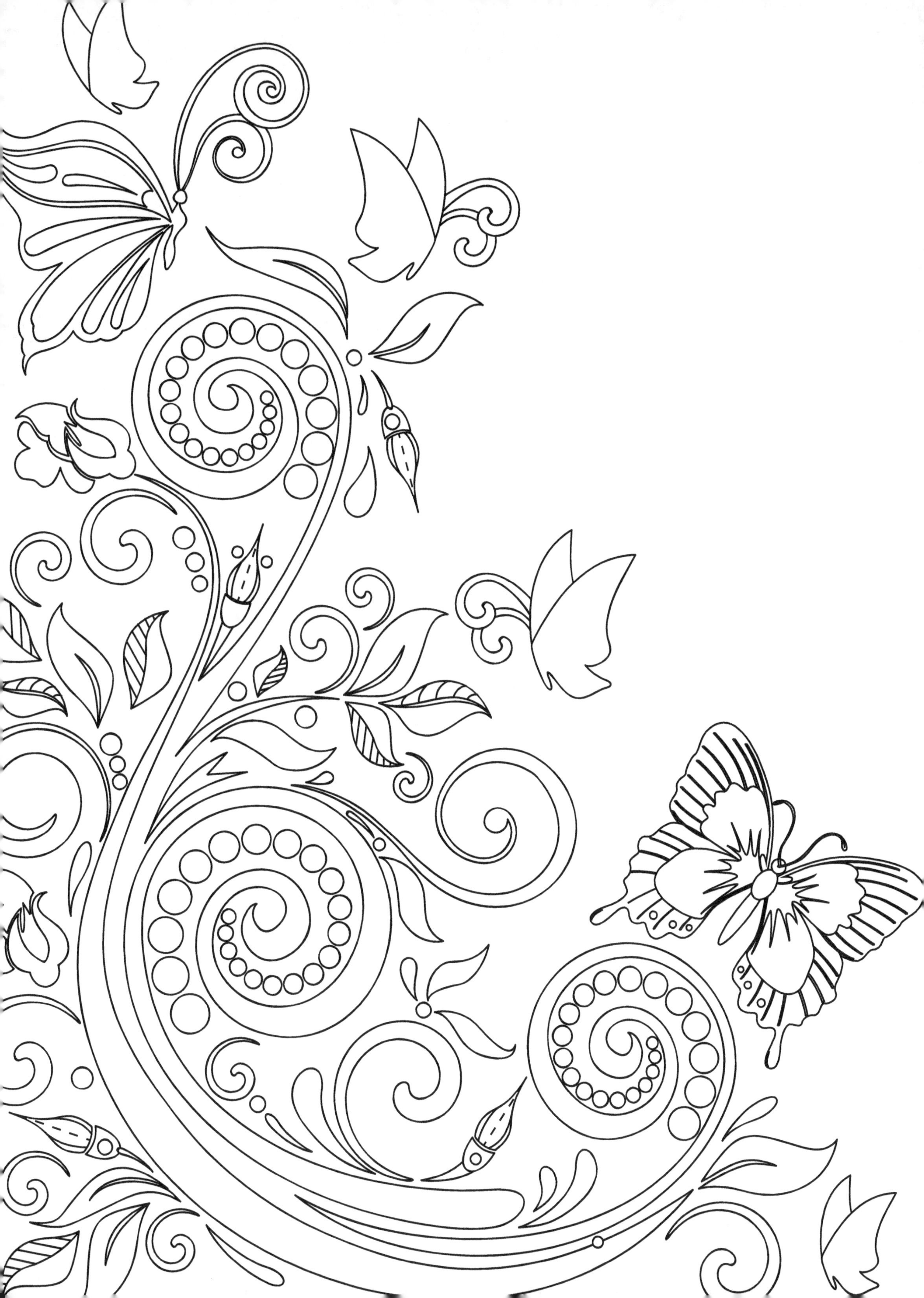

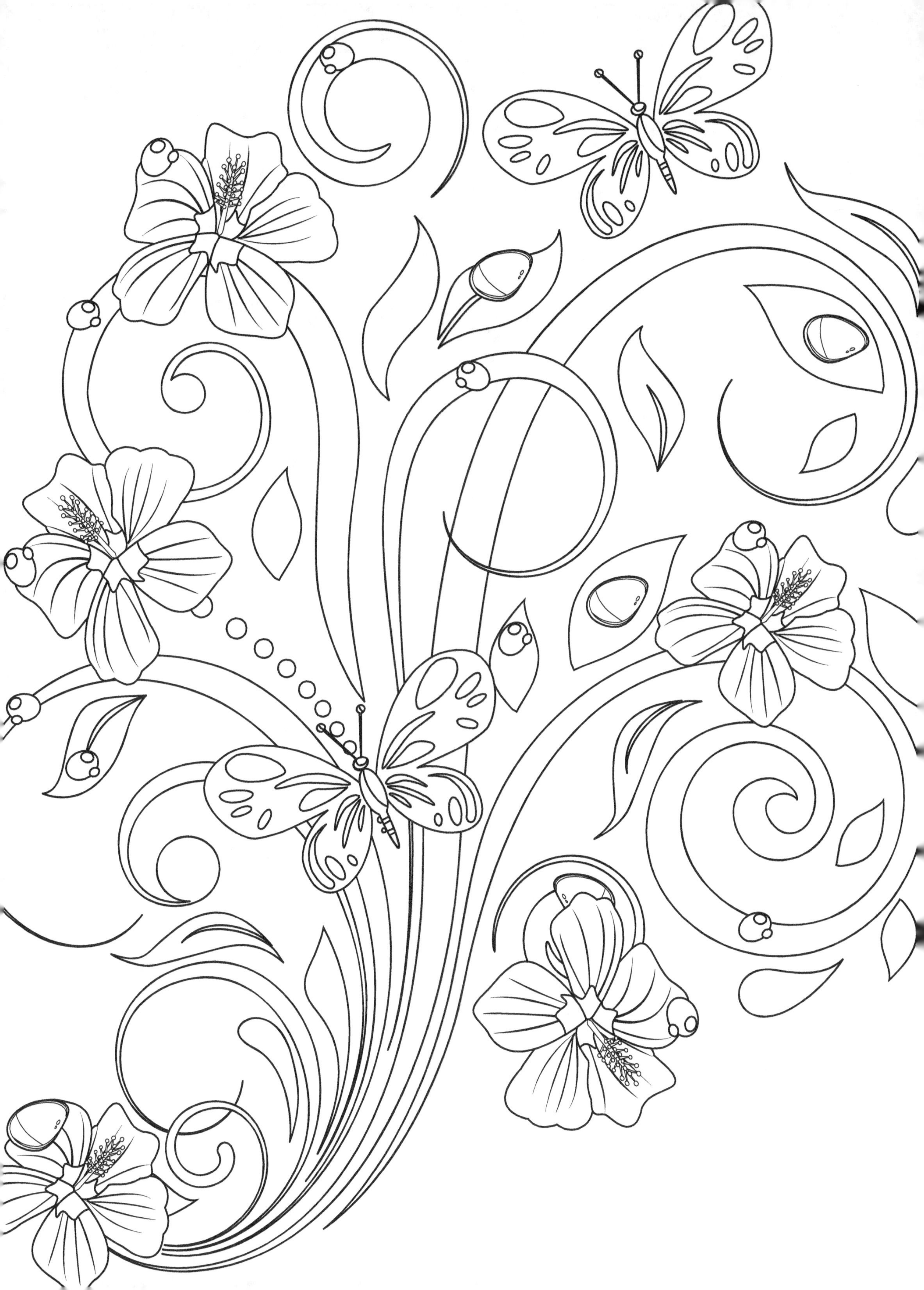

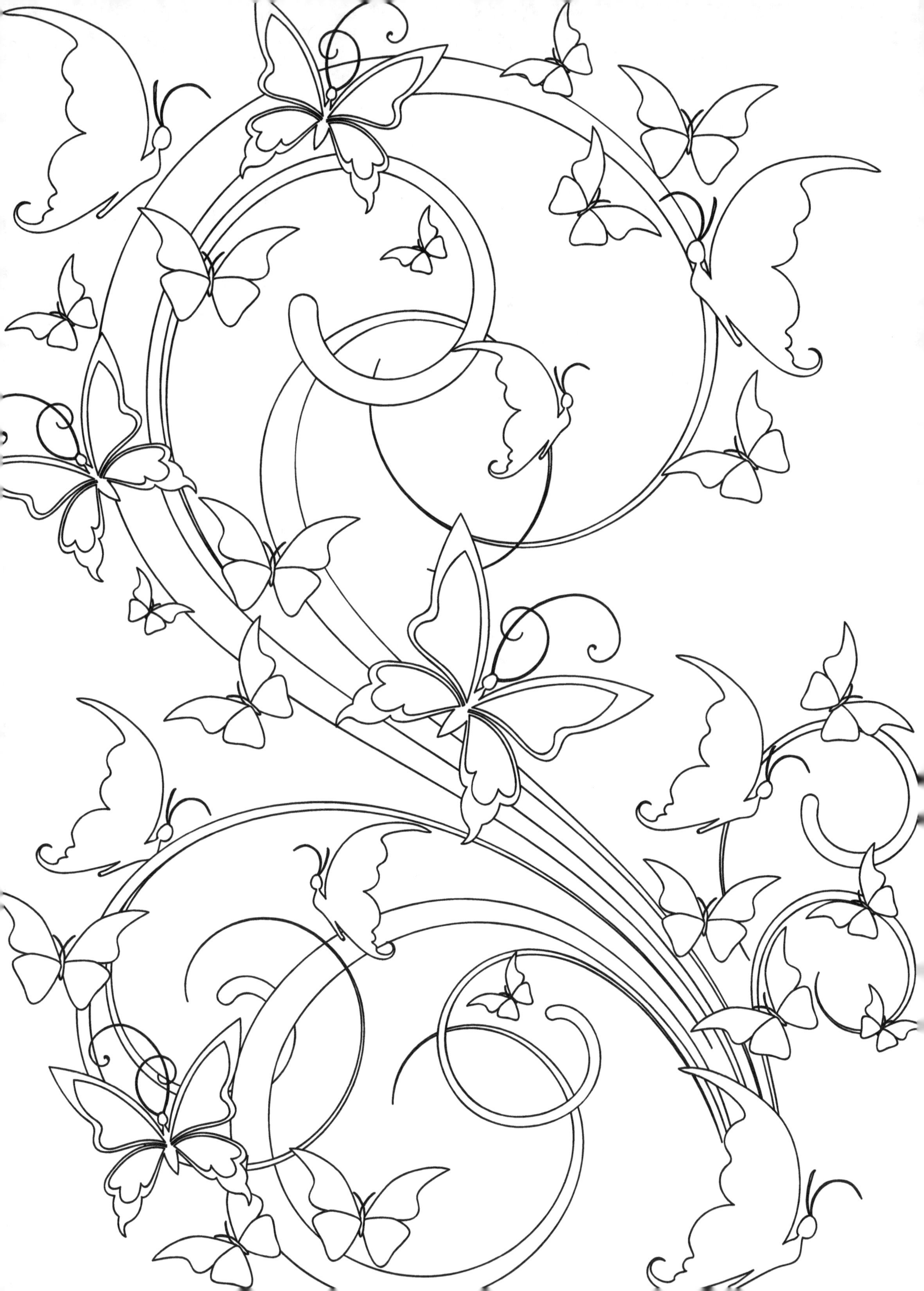

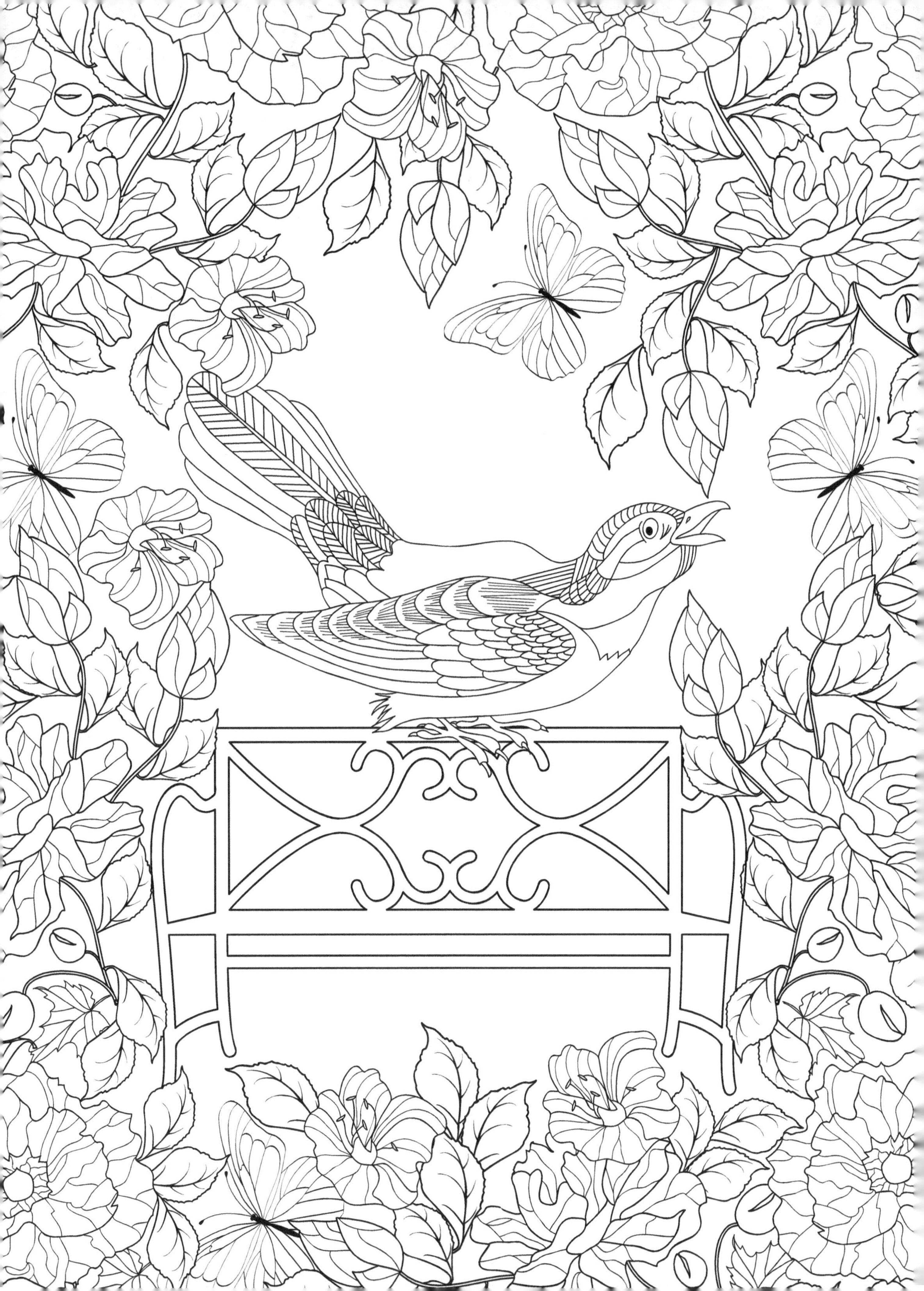

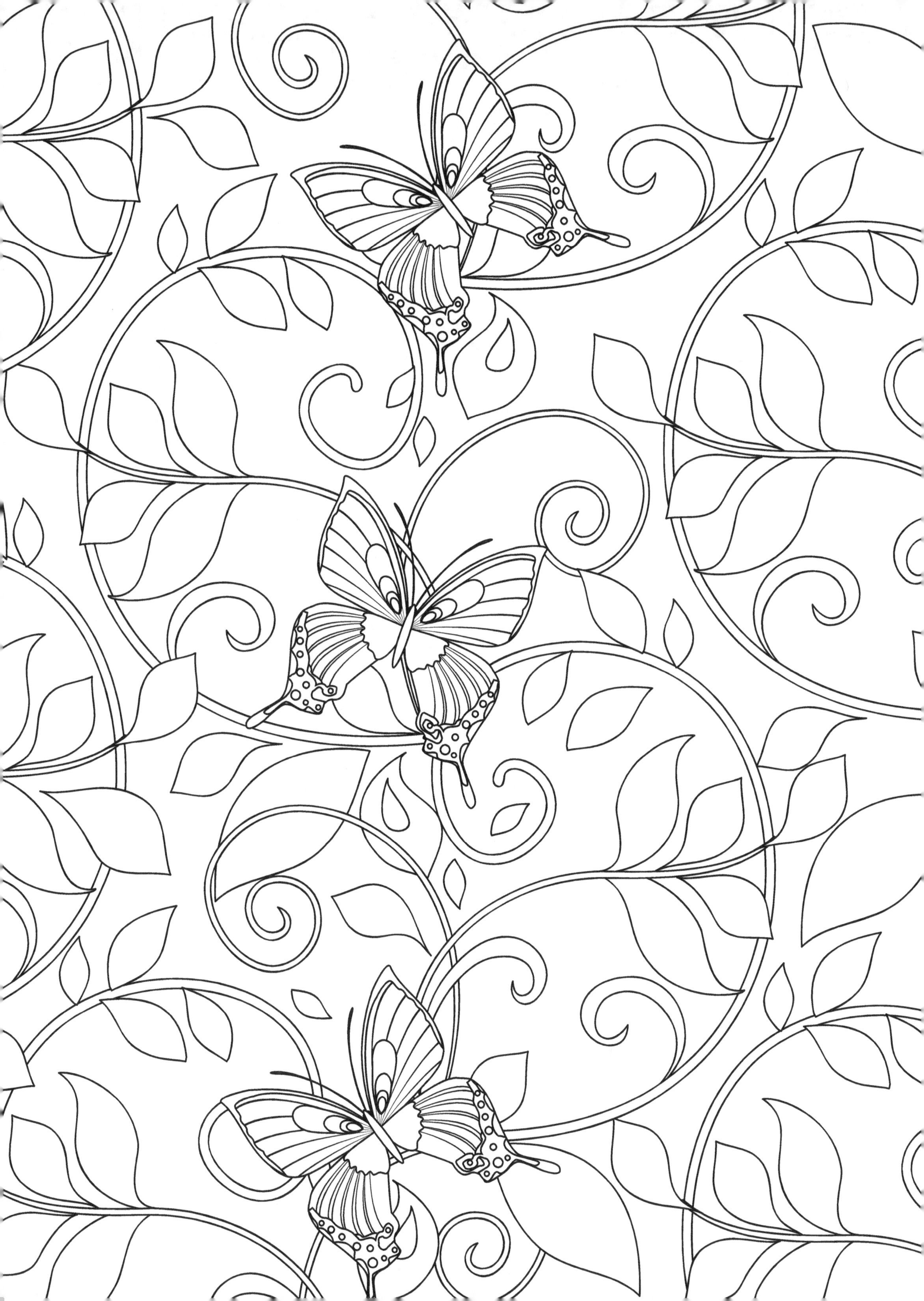

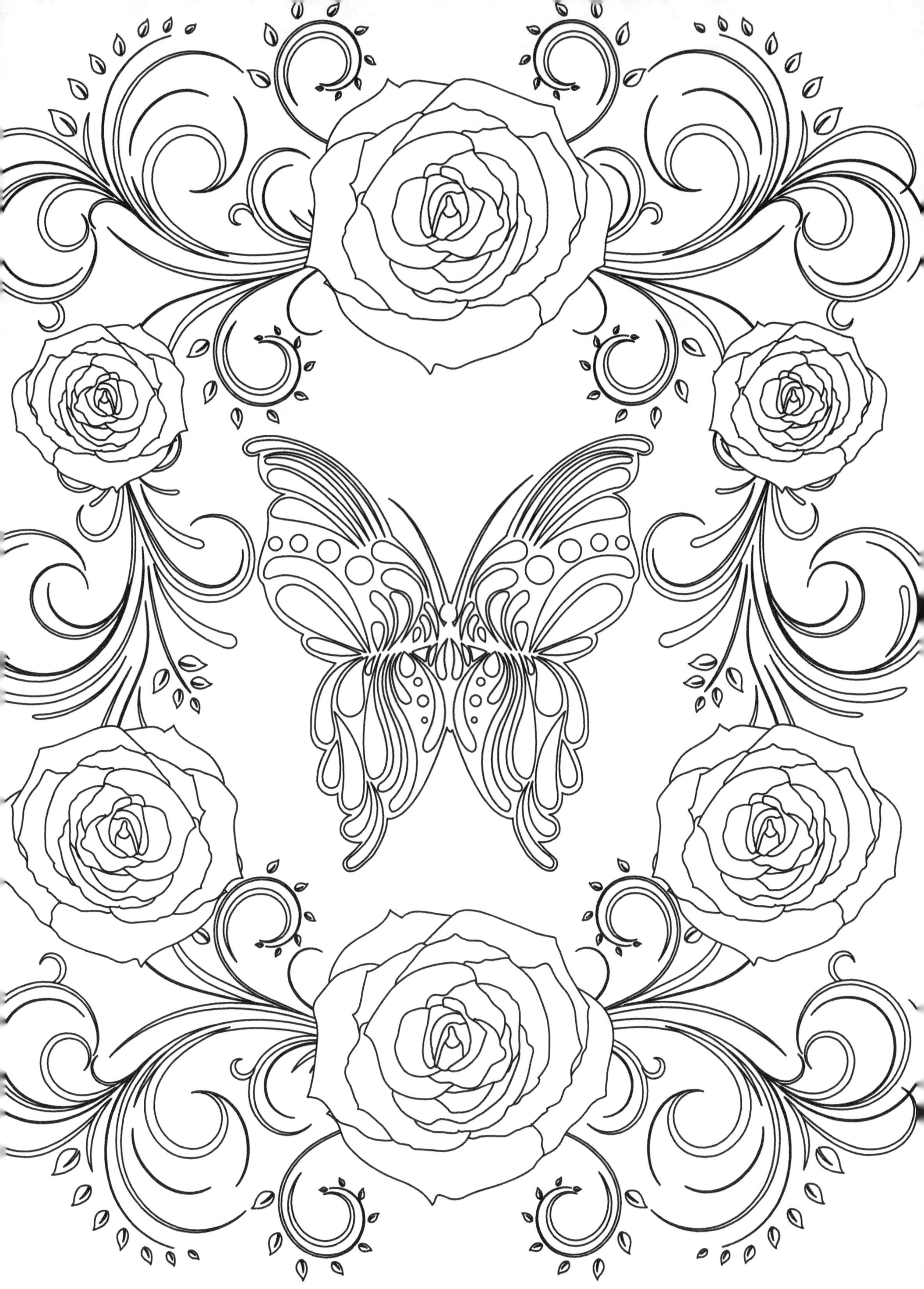

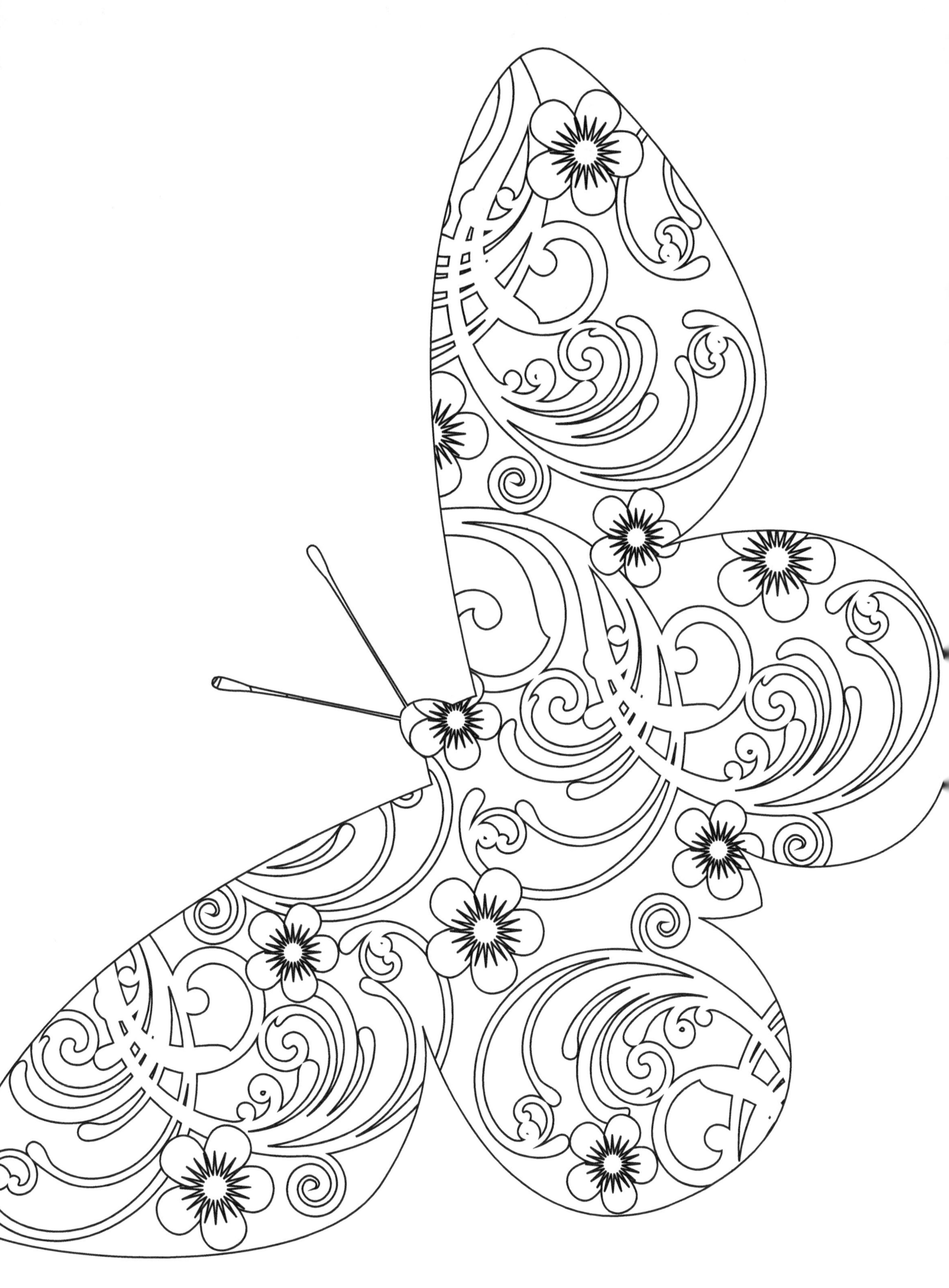

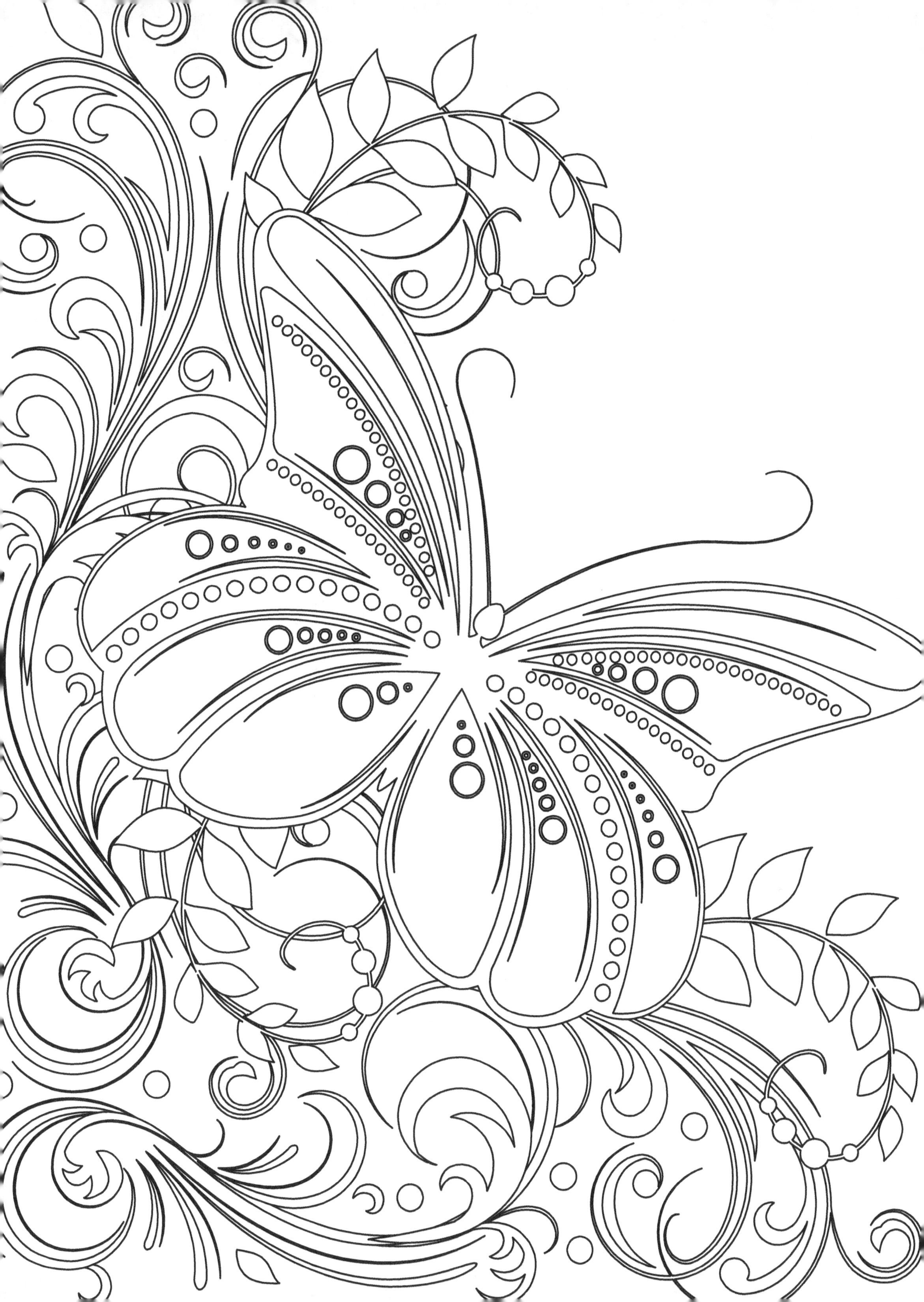

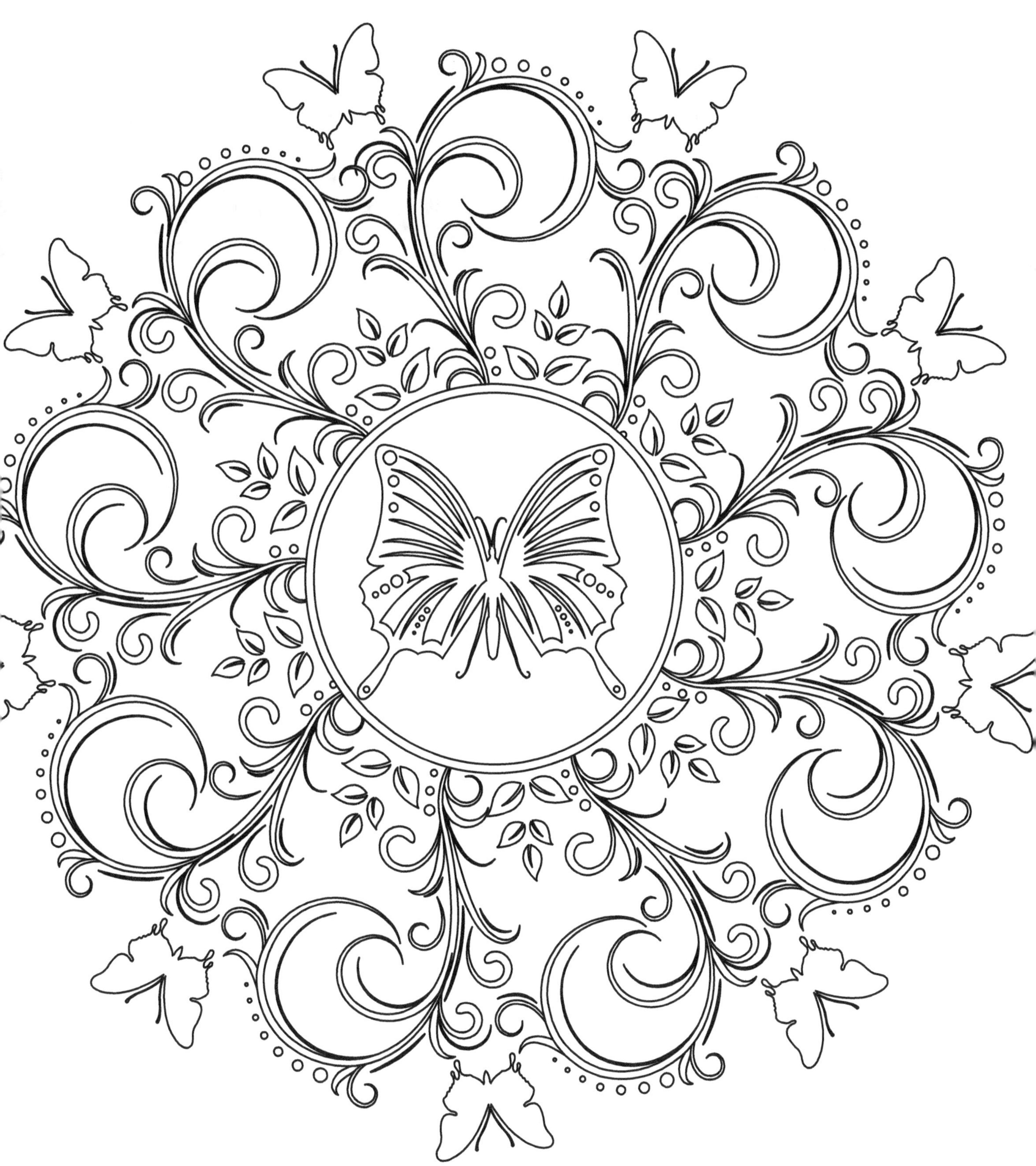

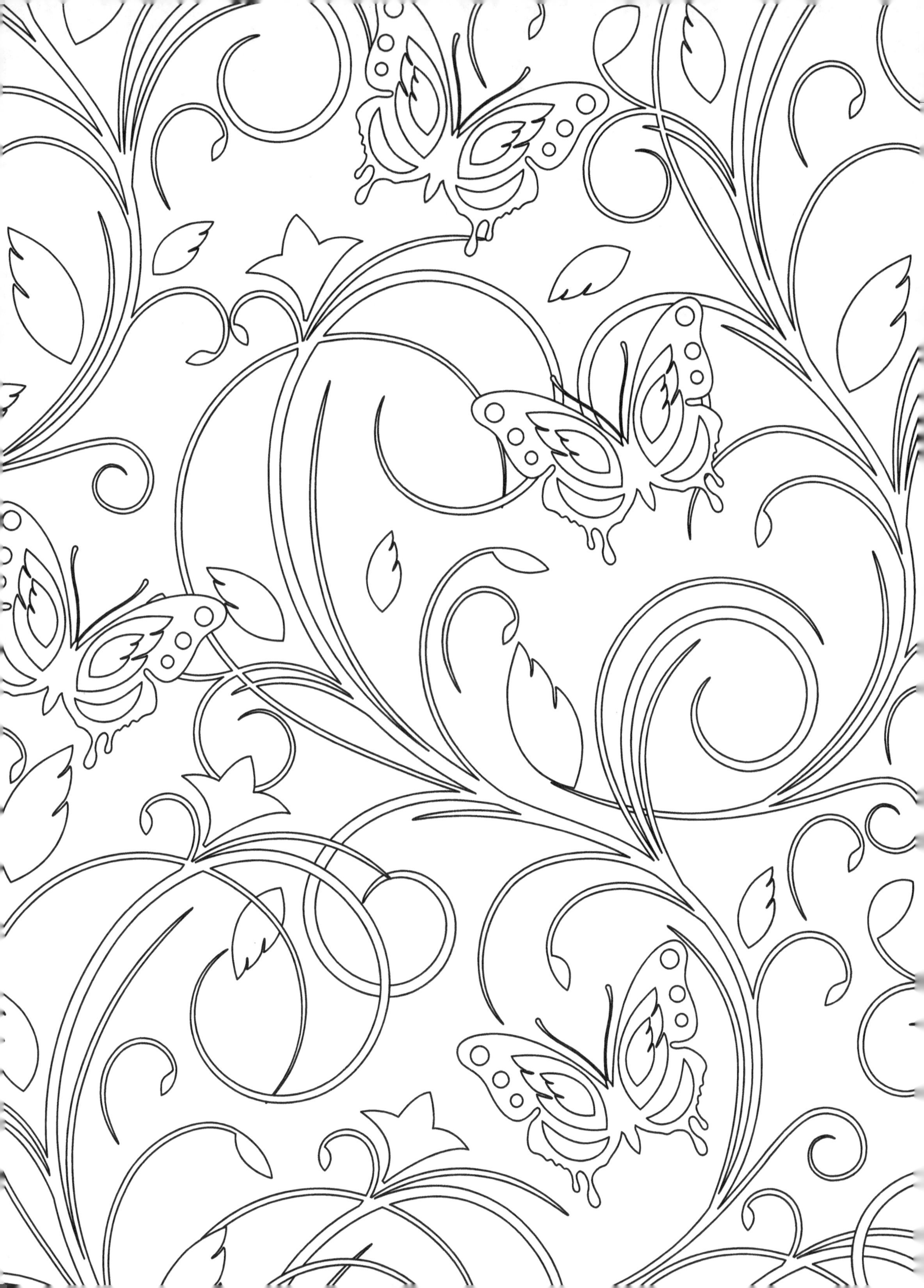

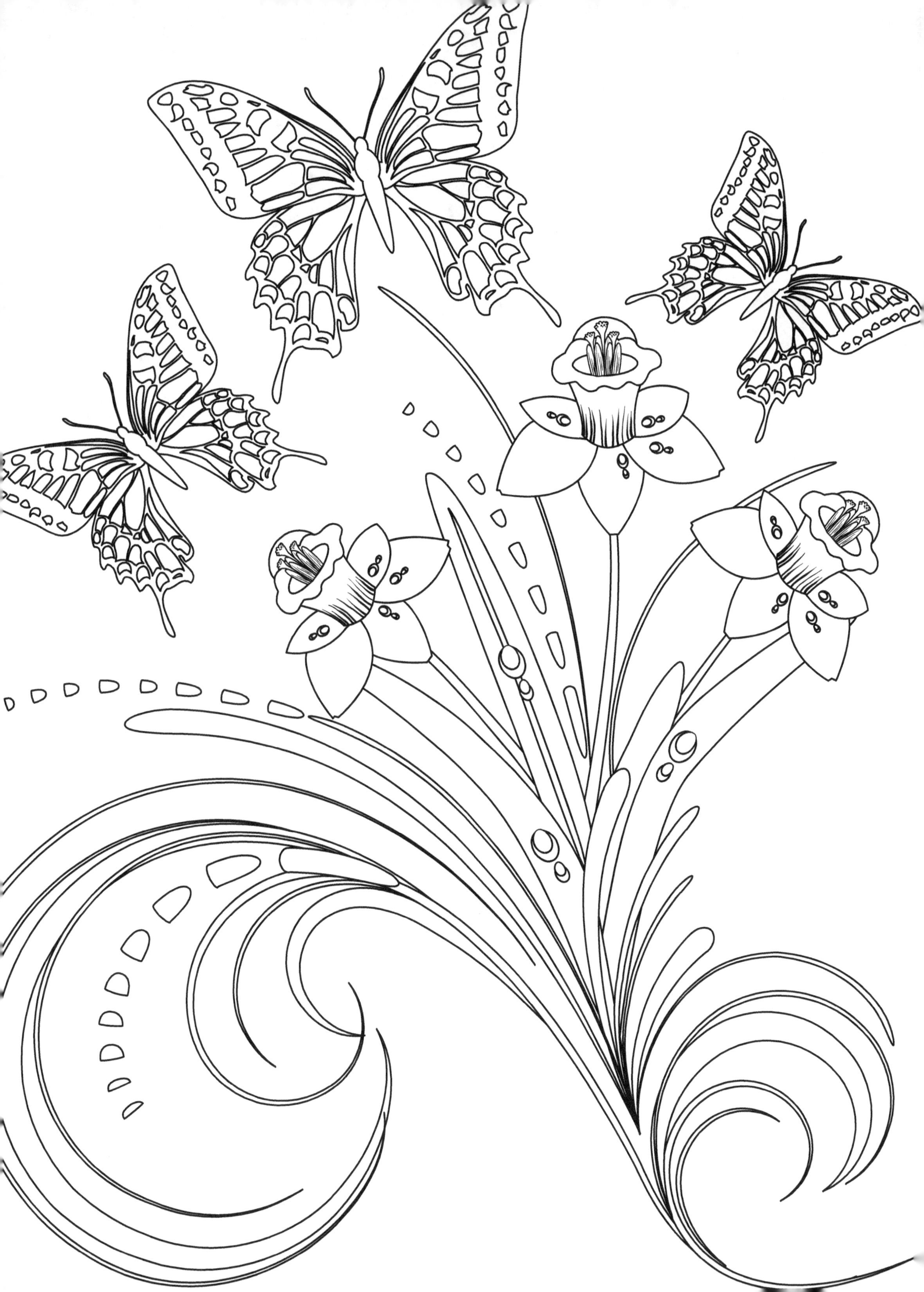

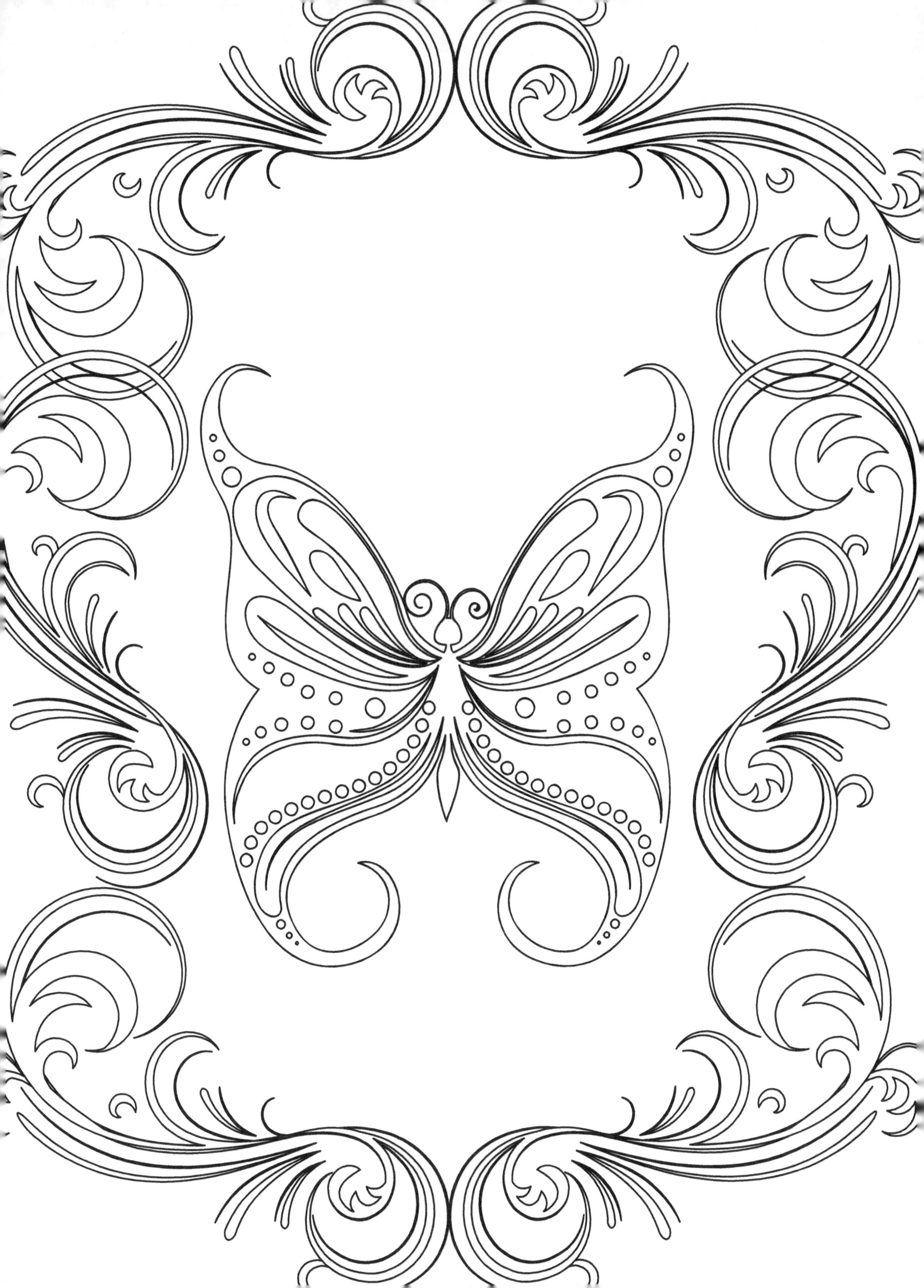

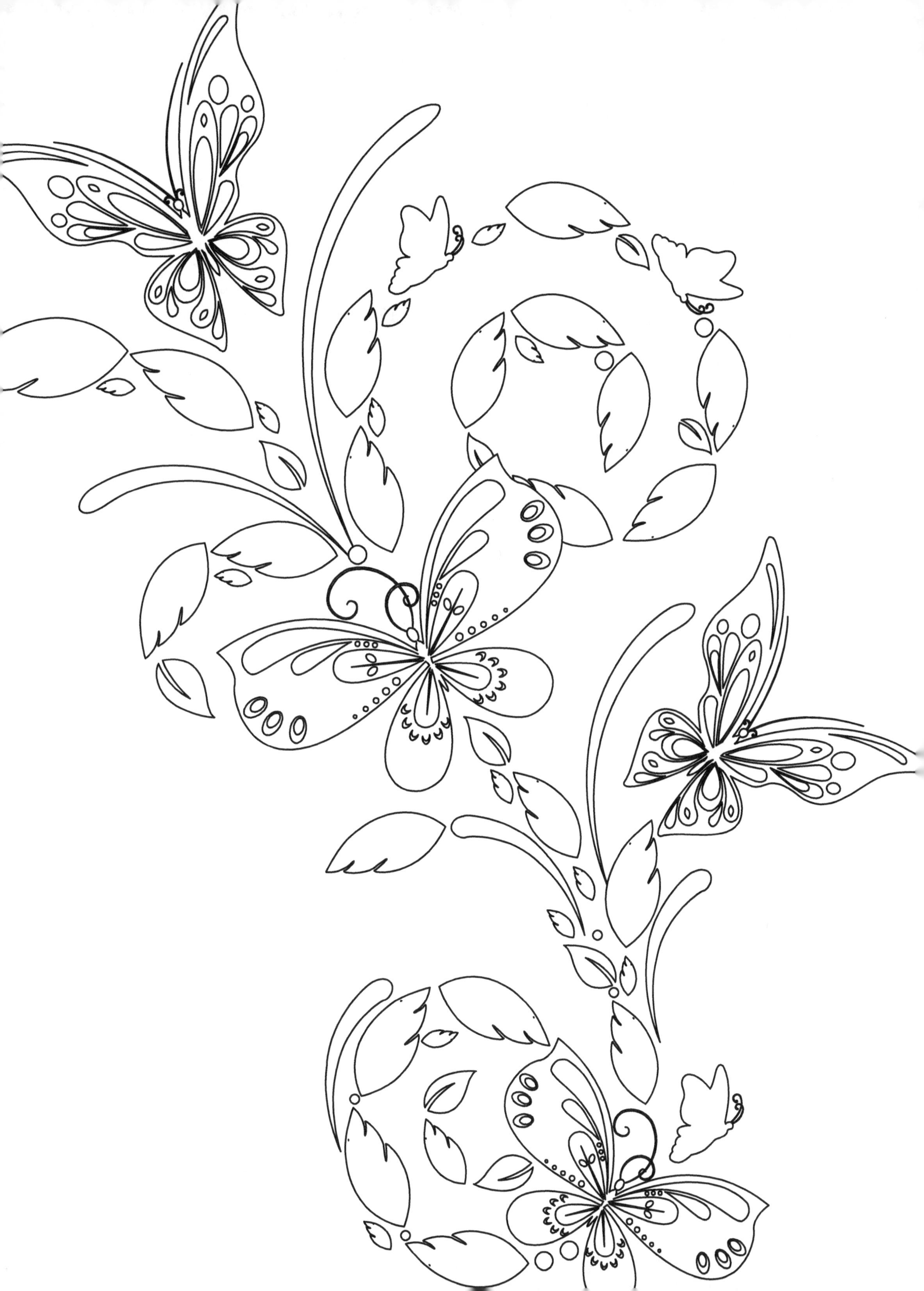

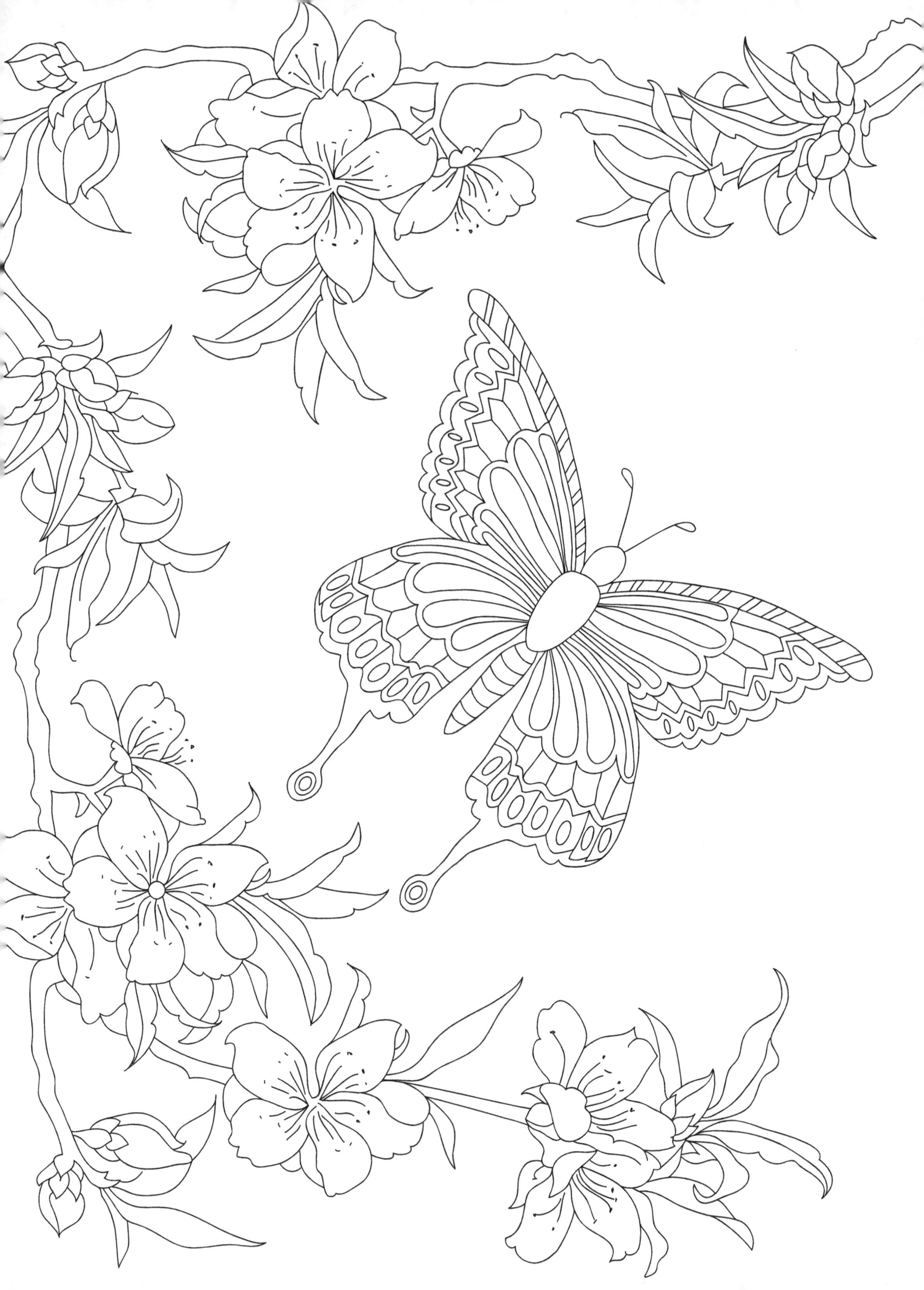

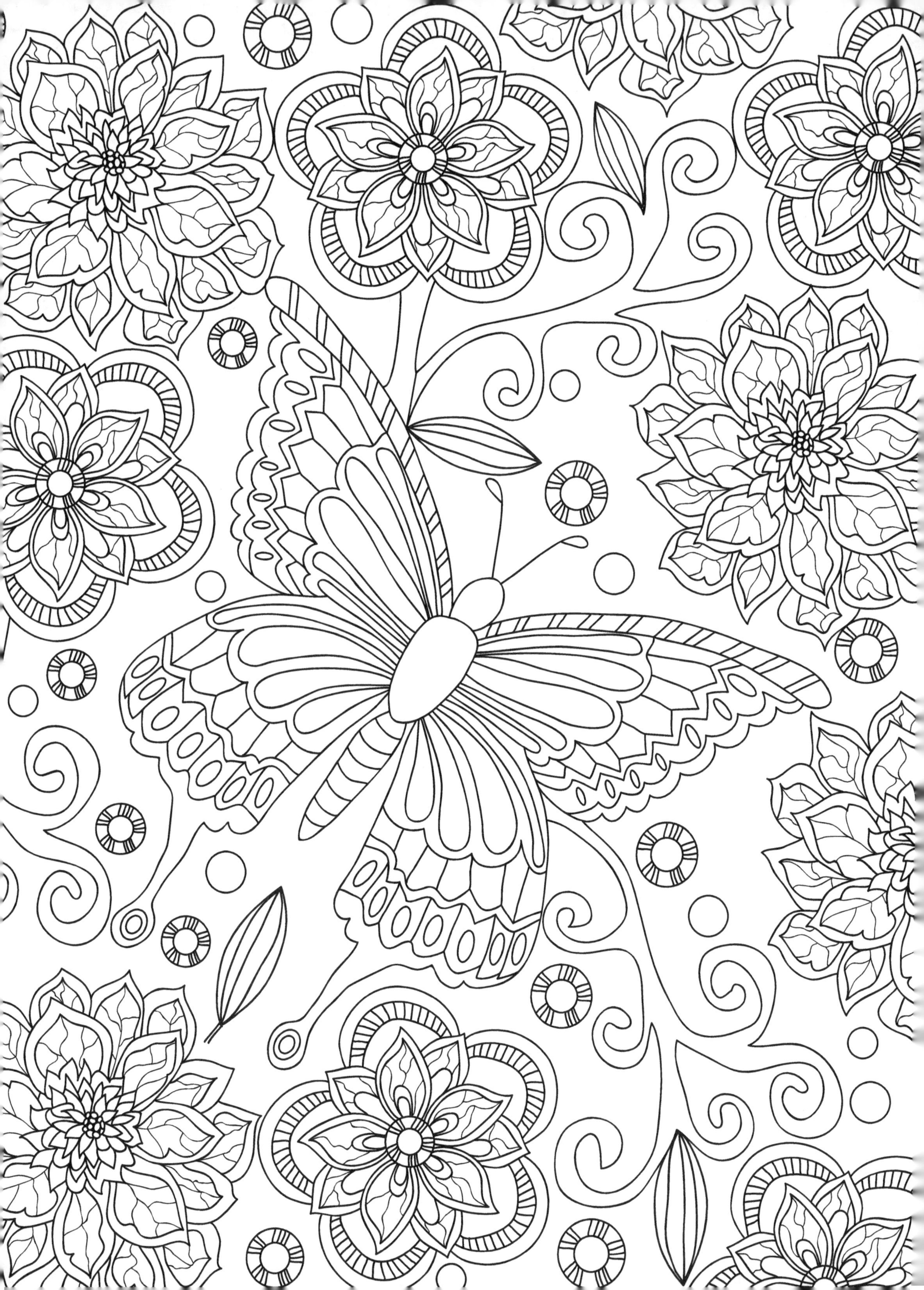

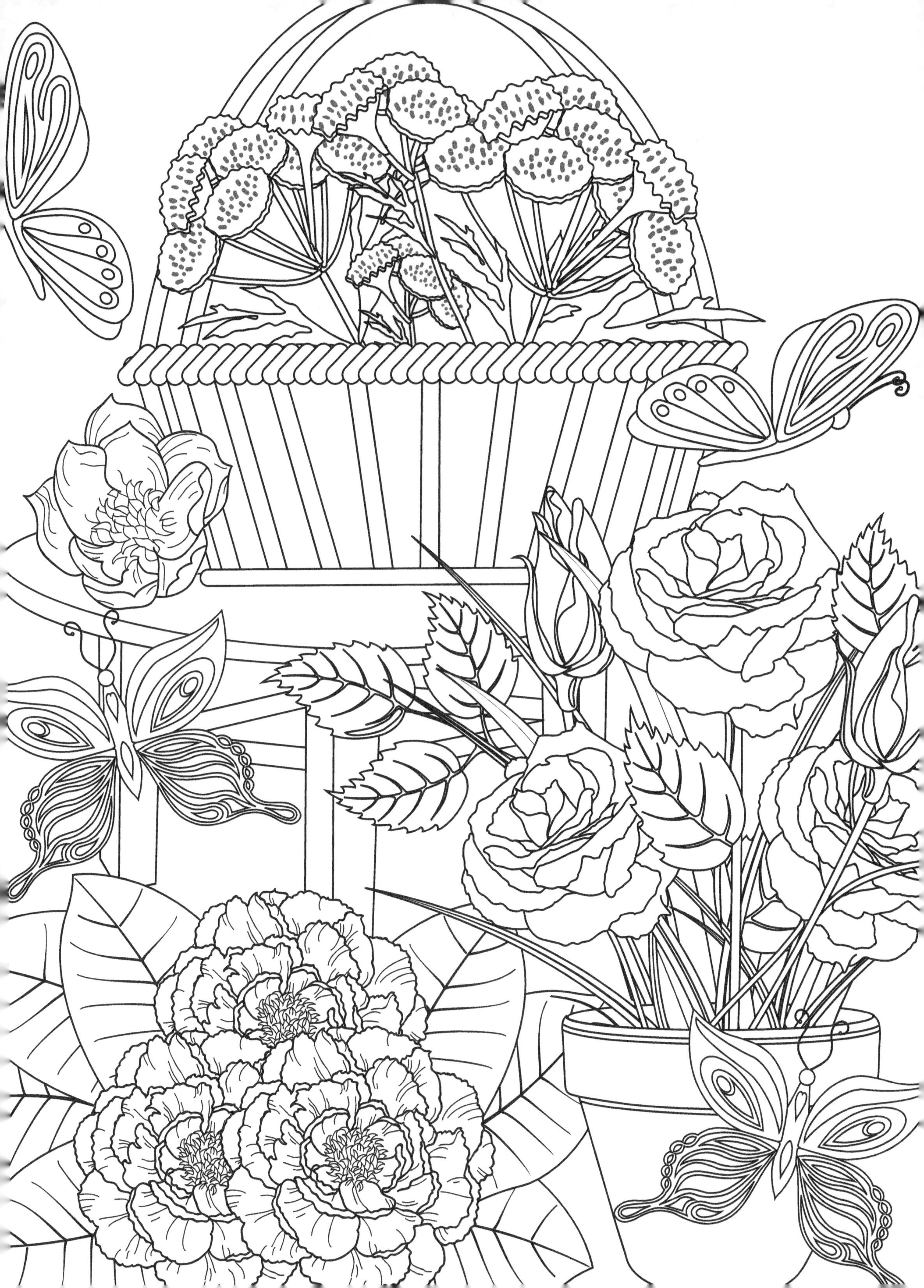

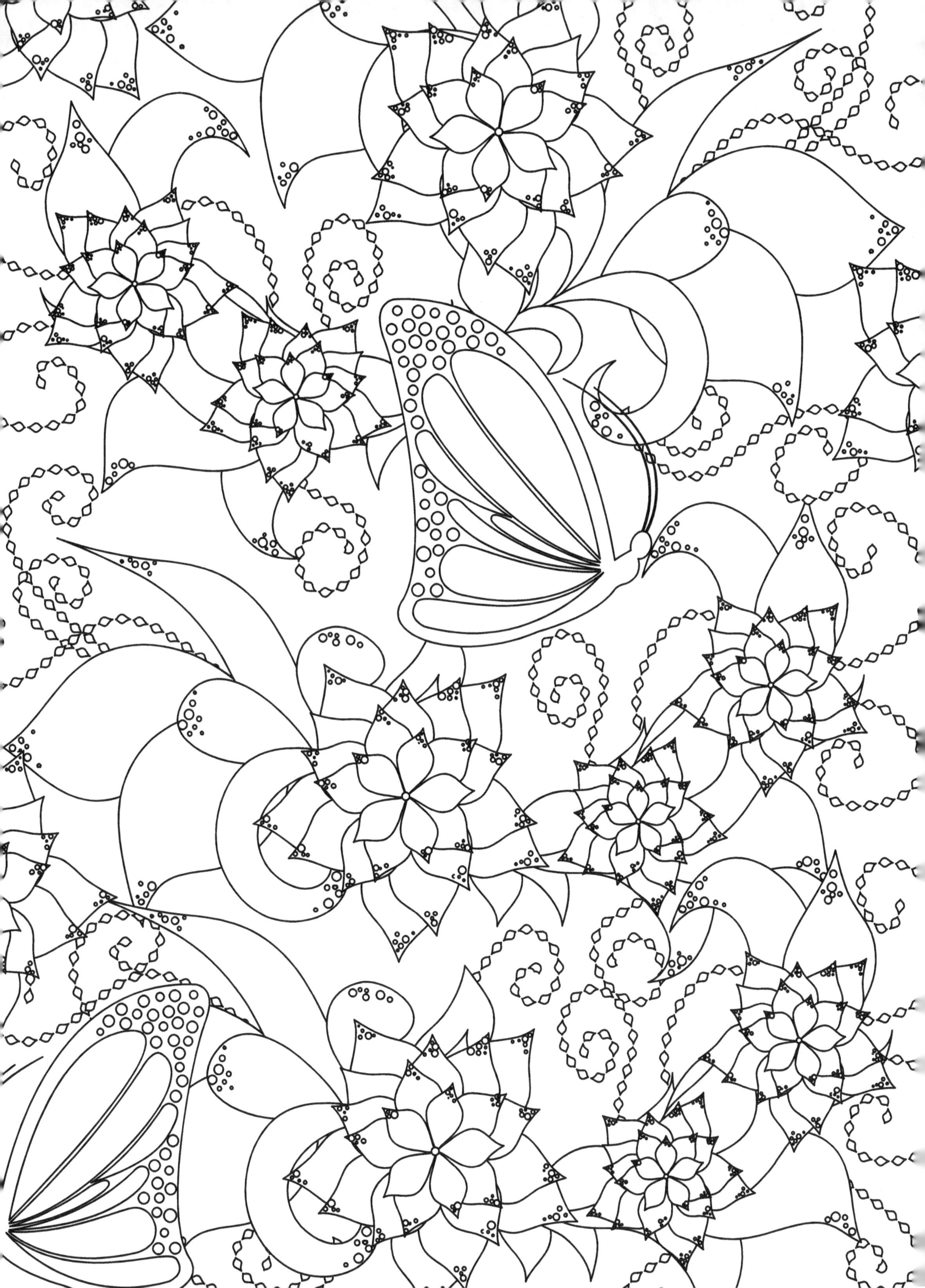

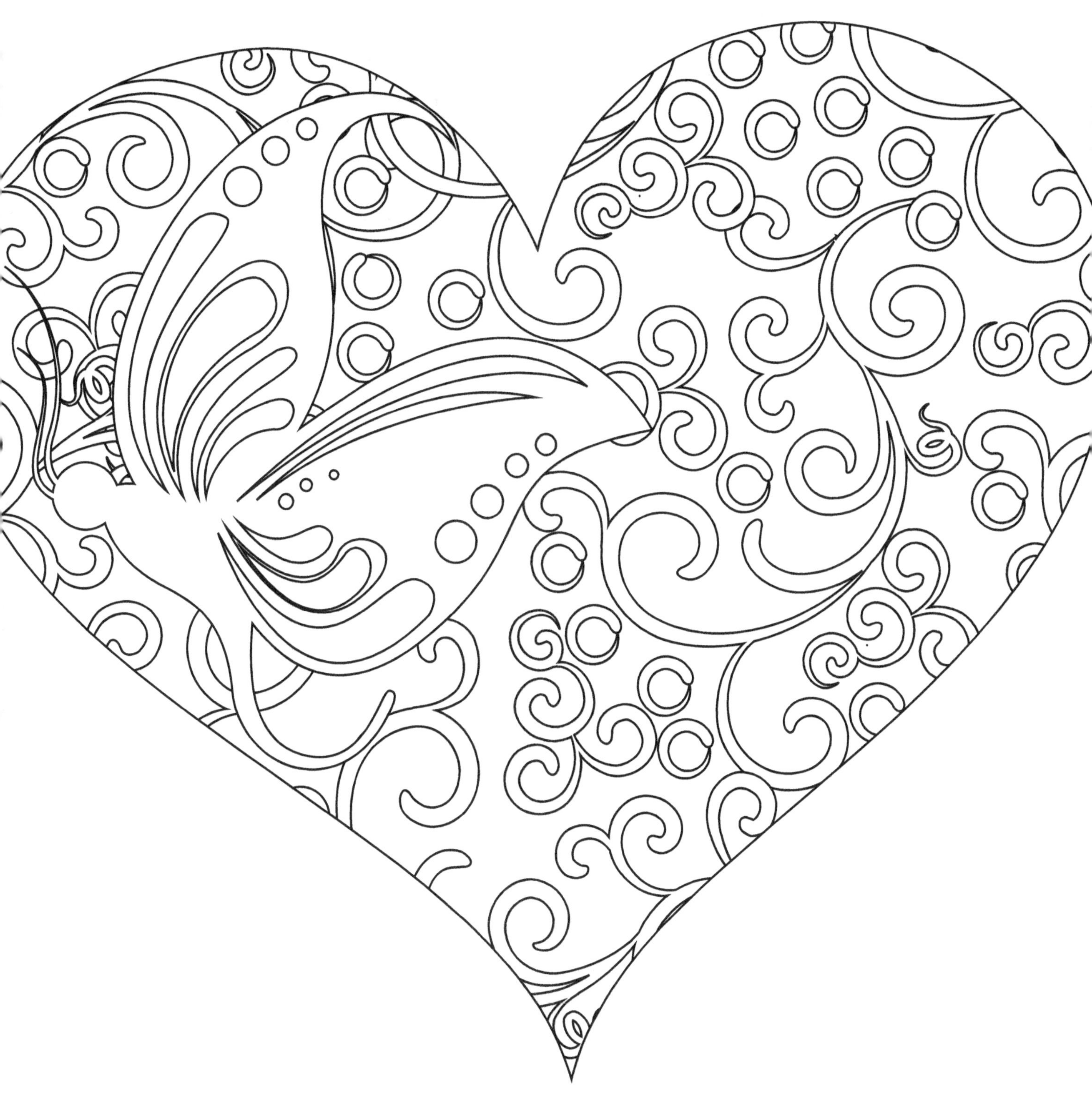

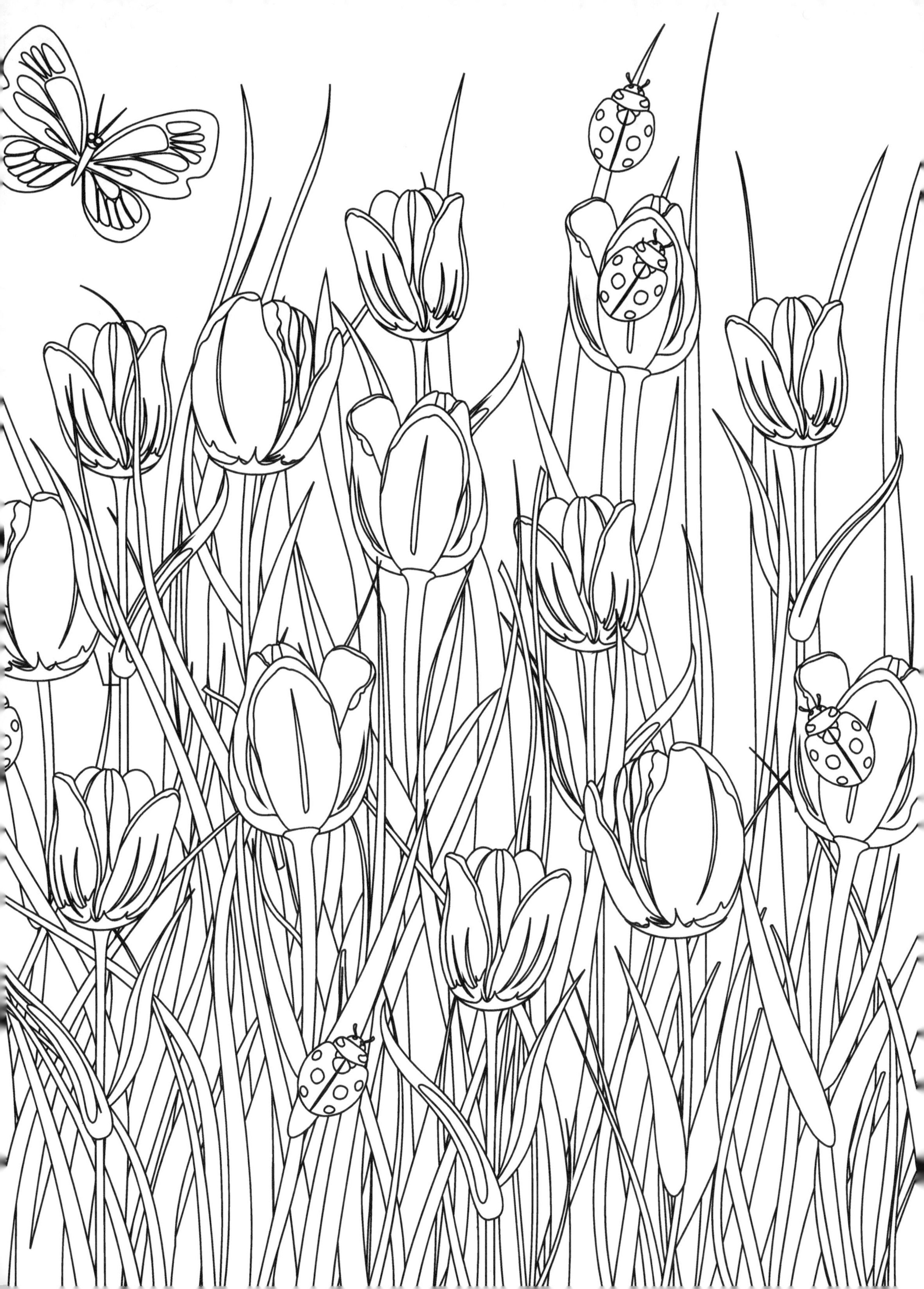

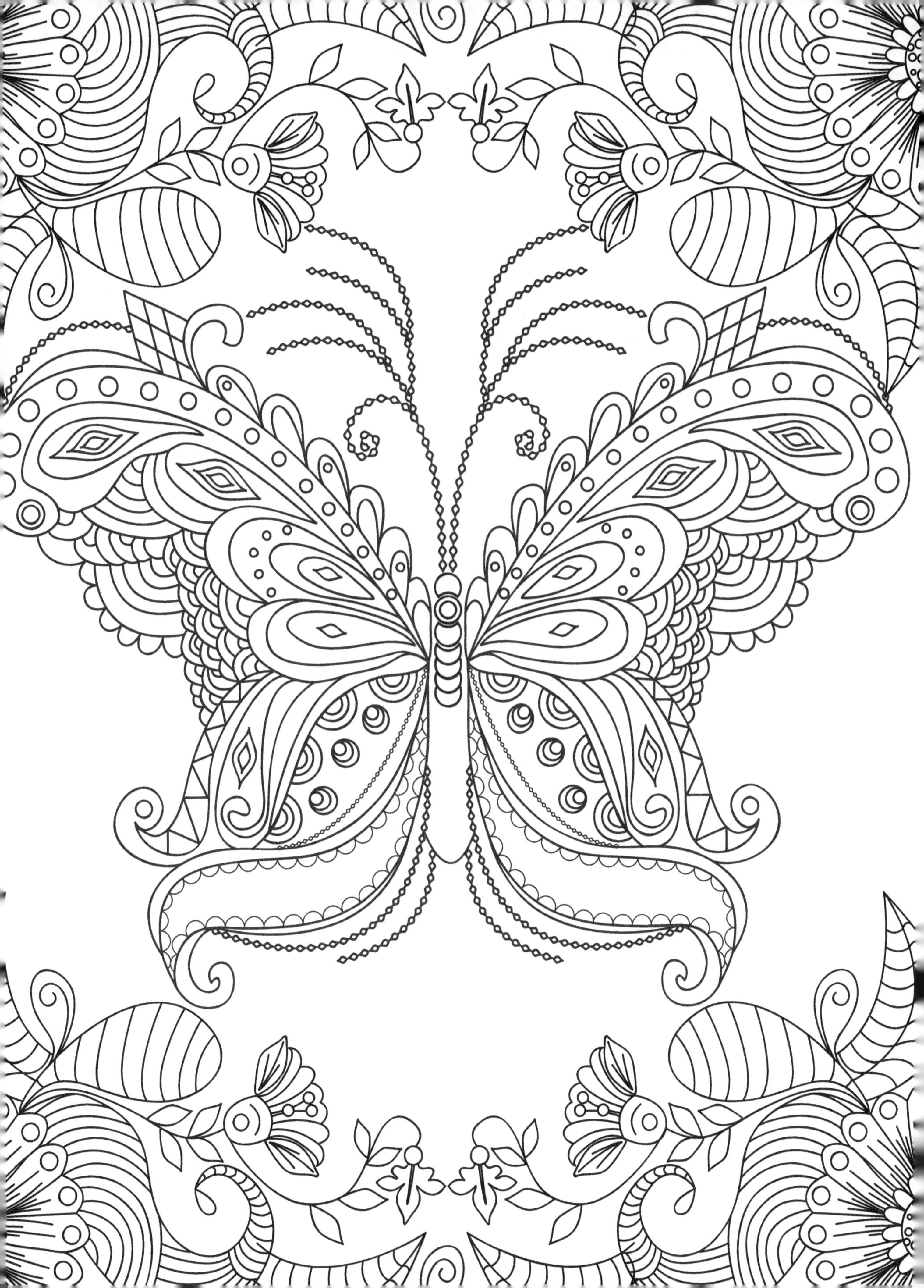

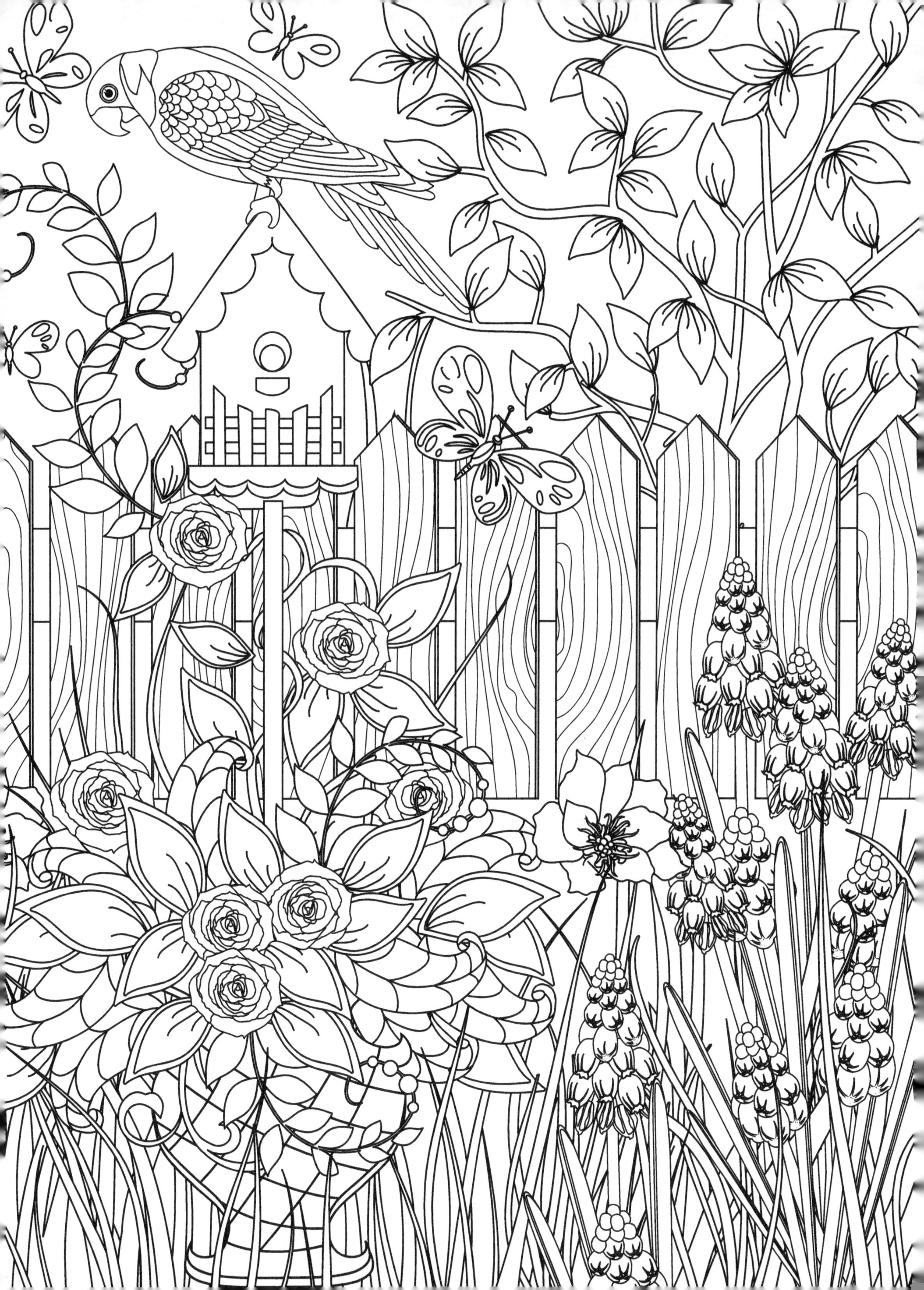

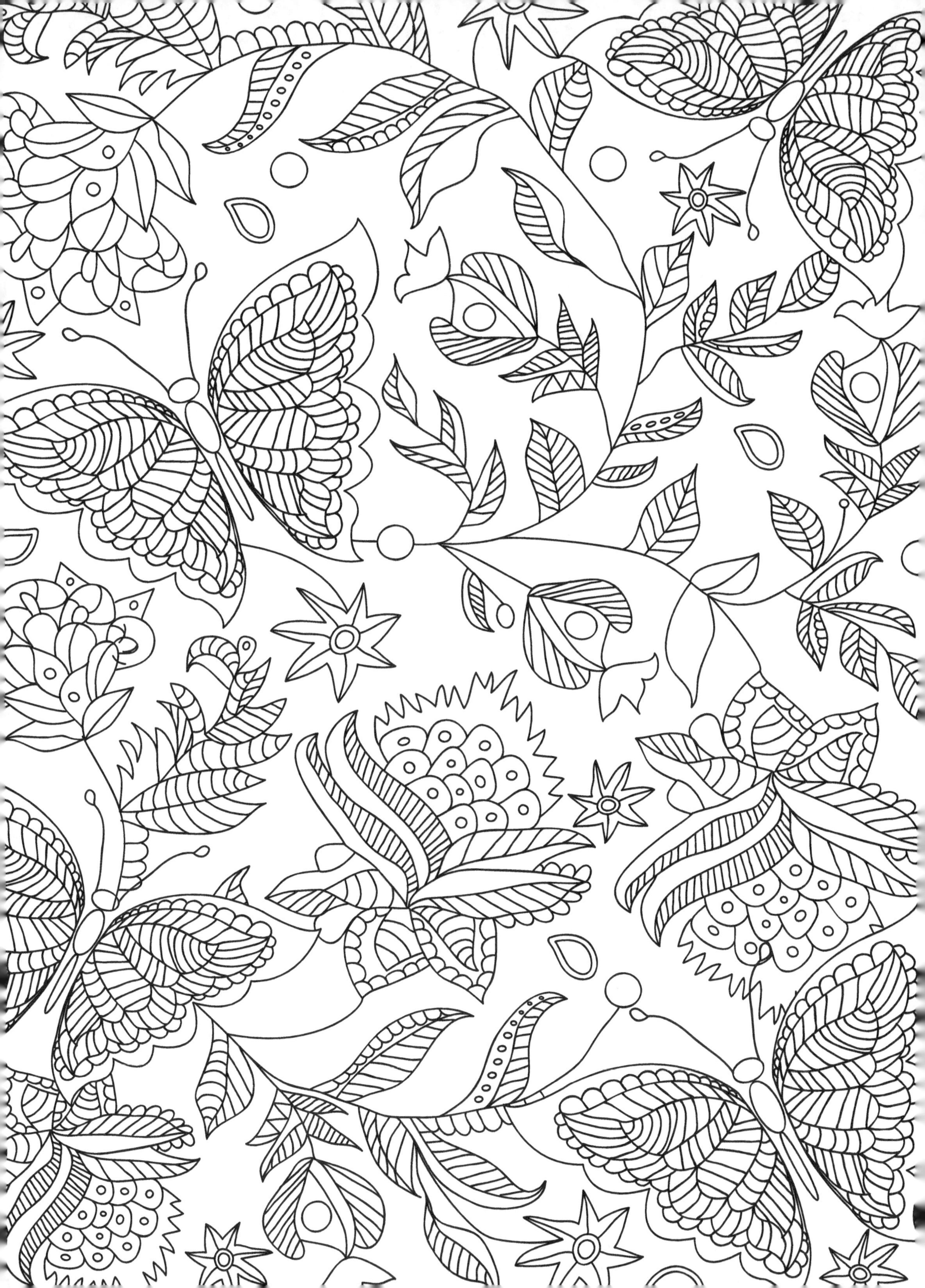

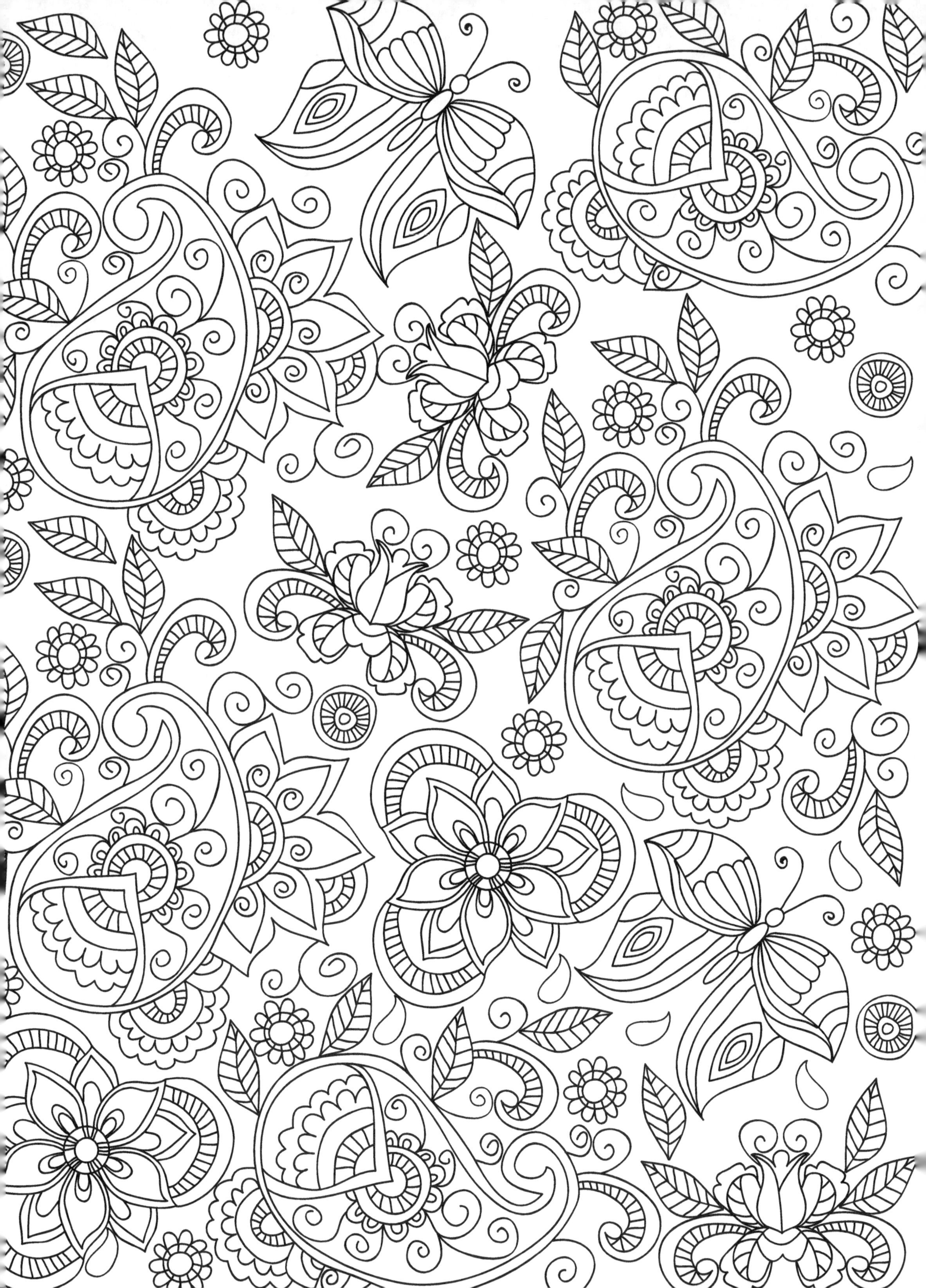